THIRD EDITION

Jack C. Richards
with Jonathan Hull and Susan Proctor

WORKBOOK

CAMBRIDGE UNIVERSITY PRESS
Cambridge, New York, Melbourne, Madrid, Cape Town, Singapore, São Paulo

Cambridge University Press
40 West 20th Street, New York, NY 10011–4211, USA

www.cambridge.org
Information on this title: www.cambridge.org/9780521602228

© Cambridge University Press 2005

This book is in copyright. Subject to statutory exception
and to the provisions of relevant collective licensing agreements,
no reproduction of any part may take place without
the written permission of Cambridge University Press.

First published 2005
4th printing 2005
Interchange Third Edition Workbook 3 has been developed from *New Interchange* Workbook 3,
first published by Cambridge University Press in 1998.

Printed in Hong Kong, China

A catalog record for this publication is available from the British Library

ISBN-13 978-0-521-60222-8 Workbook
ISBN-10 0-521-60222-X Workbook

Cambridge University Press has no responsibility for
the persistence or accuracy of URLs for external or
third-party Internet Web sites referred to in this book,
and does not guarantee that any content on such
Web sites is, or will remain, accurate or appropriate.

Art direction, book design, photo research, and layout services: Adventure House, NYC

Contents

	Acknowledgments	*iv*
1	That's what friends are for!	*1*
2	Career moves	*7*
3	Could you do me a favor?	*13*
4	What a story!	*19*
5	Crossing cultures	*25*
6	What's wrong with it?	*31*
7	The world we live in	*37*
8	Lifelong learning	*43*
9	At your service	*49*
10	The past and the future	*55*
11	Life's little lessons	*61*
12	The right stuff	*67*
13	That's a possibility.	*73*
14	Behind the scenes	*79*
15	There should be a law!	*85*
16	Challenges and accomplishments	*91*

Acknowledgments

Illustrations

Tim Foley 22, 26
Travis Foster 14, 88
Jeff Grunewald 31 (*no. 2*), 54 (*nos. 1, 3, 4, 5*)
Randy Jones 1, 4, 6, 7, 10, 16, 18, 20, 25, 28, 29, 33, 44, 50, 51, 64, 65, 66, 73, 78, 85, 87, 96

Mark Kaufman 31 (*all except no. 2*), 34, 54 (*nos. 2, 6*)
Ben Shannon 5, 84, 90, 94
Kevin Spaulding 13 (*bottom*)
Sam Viviano 8, 13 (*top*), 15, 23, 53, 59, 62, 76, 77, 86

Photo credits

2 © Jason Homa/Getty Images
9 (*left to right, top to bottom*) © Michael Nelson/Getty Images; © Patti & Milt Putnam/Corbis; © Morris Lane/Corbis; © Jo Hale/Getty Images; © Ariel Skelley/Corbis; © Lonnie Duka/Index Stock
12 (*clockwise from top left*) © Joe Cornish/Getty Images; © Picture Quest; © Stephen Simpson/Getty Images; © Peter Steiner/Getty Images
17 © Dex Images, Inc./Corbis
19 (*top to bottom*) © Telegraph Colour Library/Getty Images; © M.P. Kahl/Photo Researchers
21 © Robert Ketchum
24 (*left to right*) © Michael Paras/International Stock Photography; © Jose L. Pelaez/Corbis; © James Davis/International Stock Photography; © Dan Bosler/Getty Images; © Dan Bosler/Getty Images
30 © Marc Serota/Reuters/Corbis
32 (*left to right*) © Getty Images; © Jackson Smith/Uniphoto
38 © William B. Folsom/Uniphoto
39 Courtesy of Greenpeace
40 © Nick David/Photonica
41 © Max Hilaire/Getty Images
42 © A. Ramey/PhotoEdit
43 © David Young-Wolff/PhotoEdit
45 © James Davis/International Stock Photography
46 © Ron Chapple/Getty Images; © Erik Dreyer/Getty Images; © Think Stock
47 © Don Smetzer/Getty Images; © Amwell/Getty Images; © Michael Phillip Manheim/International Stock Photography; © Robert E. Daemmrich/Getty Images
48 (*top to bottom*) © Ursula Markus/Photo Researchers; © Rob Lewine/Corbis
49 (*top to bottom*) © Phil Cantor/Index Stock; © Getty Images; © David Oliver/Getty Images
52 © Bridget Morley from page 139 of "The Personal Feng Shui Manual" by permission of Gai Books Ltd., London
55 (*top to bottom*) © Archive Photos/Frank Driggs Collection; © Tom Stoddart/Katz/Woodfin Camp & Associates

56 (*top to bottom*) © Archive Photos; © John Beatty/Photo Researchers
57 © Dr. A.C. Twomey/Photo Researchers
58 (*top to bottom*) © David Hardy/Science Photo Library/Photo Researchers; © Ed Wheeler/Corbis
60 (*top*) © Jose Pelaez Photography/Corbis; (*bottom, left to right*) © PunchStock; © Stockbyte; © Brand X Pictures/Alamy
61 © Bob Daemmrich/PhotoEdit
63 © Franck Fife/AFP/Getty Images
67 © R. Ian Lloyd/Masterfile
68 © Chet Gordon/ImageWorks
69 (*left to right, top to bottom*) © Thinkstock; © Robert Brenner/PhotoEdit; © Richard Klune/Corbis; © Paul Almasy/Corbis; © Digital Vision; © age Fotostock
70 © Mark H. Milstein/Northfoto/Newscom
71 (*clockwise from top left*) © Advertisement used with permission from Ford; © advertisement used with permission from Kraft Foods; © advertisement used with permission from the American Automobile Association
74 (*top to bottom*) © Harald Sund/Getty Images; © Bettmann/Corbis; © Bettmann/Corbis
75 © Robert Hutchinson/Getty Images; (*inset*) © Keystone/Getty Images
79 (*left to right*) © Lynn Goldsmith/Corbis; © Christopher Weil/Corbis
80 (*left*) © Paul Howell/Getty Images; (*all others*) © Gooseberry Farms, Westport, MA
81 © NMPFT/Topham-HIP/ImageWorks
82 (*left to right*) © Robert Nickelsberg/Getty Images; © Jeff Greenberg/ImageWorks
83 © Koren Ziv/Corbis Sygma
89 © Jim Hodson/FSG/Gamma Liaison
92 (*left to right*) © Mugshots/Corbis; © John Olsen/Corbis
93 © Yannis Kontos/Corbis Sygma
94 © Shin In Sup/Joongangilbo/EPN/Newscom
95 © Alamy

1 That's what friends are for!

1 Complete these descriptions with the words from the list.

1. My roommate is pretty _____intolerant_____ .
   He's really close-minded and always has to have his way.
2. The Chans like meeting new people and having friends over for dinner. They're one of the most _____ couples I know.
3. You can't trust Jane. She always promises to do something, and then she never does it. She's pretty _____ .
4. John is so _____ ! He always has such great ideas and never takes any credit for them.
5. I never know how to act around Tina! One minute she's in a good mood, and the next minute, she's in a bad mood. She's so _____ .

☑ intolerant
☐ modest
☐ temperamental
☐ sociable
☐ unreliable

2 Opposites

A Complete the chart by forming the opposites of the adjectives in the list. Use *in-* and *un-*. Then check your answers in a dictionary.

☑ ambitious   ☐ dependent   ☐ popular   ☐ sensitive
☐ attractive   ☐ experienced   ☐ reasonable   ☐ sociable
☑ competent   ☐ formal   ☐ reliable   ☐ tolerant

incompetent

Opposites with *in-*	Opposites with *un-*
incompetent	unambitious

B Write four sentences using any of the words in part A.

Example: *Fred is very ambitious at work, but he's inexperienced. He still has a lot to learn.*

1. _____
2. _____
3. _____
4. _____

3 Add who or that to the conversation where necessary. Put an X where who or that is not necessary.

A: I'm looking for someone ___**X**___ I can go on vacation with.

B: Hmm. So what kind of person are you looking for?

A: I want to travel with someone _____ is easygoing and independent.

B: Right. And you'd probably also like a person _____ is reliable.

A: Yeah, and I want someone _____ I know well.

B: So why don't you ask me?

A: You? I know you *too* well!

B: Ha! Does that mean you think I'm someone _____ is high-strung, dependent, and unreliable?

A: No! I'm just kidding. You're definitely someone _____ I could go on vacation with. So, . . . what are you doing in June?

4 Complete the sentences with who or that and your own information or ideas.

1. I generally like to go out with people <u>who are easygoing and have a sense of humor</u> .
2. I'd rather travel with someone _____ .
3. I don't really want a roommate _____ .
4. My classmates and I like teachers _____ .
5. My best friend and I want to meet people _____ .
6. Most workers would prefer a boss _____ .
7. Some people don't like stingy types _____ .
8. I don't want to have moody friends _____ .
9. I feel comfortable discussing my problems with friends _____ .
10. My favorite friends are people _____ .

5 Signs of fashion

A Do you think your sign influences the way you dress? Read the Chinese horoscope chart.

Because Chinese New Year falls in January or February, the sign for someone born in either month could be the sign for the preceding year.

The Dog
1946 1958 1970 1982 1994 2006
You like it when people like you. If you are a woman, you are neat and very stylish. If you are a man, you are no different.

The Rooster
1945 1957 1969 1981 1993 2005
Your hair is very important to you. Women who are born in these years always think first about their hair, and they don't care about their wardrobe. If you are a man, you are very similar.

The Monkey
1944 1956 1968 1980 1992 2004
If you are a woman, you have a large wardrobe, and you like to impress people with your choice of clothes. If you are a man, you don't worry too much about what you wear.

The Goat
1943 1955 1967 1979 1991 2003
If you are a woman, you love to dress in style and with taste, and you have a very large closet. If you are a man, you really like to wear designer clothes.

The Pig
1947 1959 1971 1983 1995 2007
Whether you are a man or a woman, you love dressing up. You are sociable, and you like to go to parties to show off your new clothes. If others don't notice them, you get upset.

The Horse
1942 1954 1966 1978 1990 2002
You like elegance, and you follow the latest fashions. If you are a woman, you know this already; however, if you are a man, it may take you a while to realize this.

The Rat
1948 1960 1972 1984 1996 2008
If you are a woman, you don't dress to impress people. But you like it when people notice your charm. If you are a man, you often wear what you threw on the floor the night before.

The Snake
1941 1953 1965 1977 1989 2001
Women like to wear a lot of jewelry and other accessories. If you are a man, you think carefully about what you wear, and you have very good taste.

The Buffalo
1949 1961 1973 1985 1997 2009
You are a practical woman. You like to wear functional clothes during the day and dress much more colorfully at night. If you are a man, you are simply not interested in clothes.

The Tiger
1950 1962 1974 1986 1998 2010
You are the kind of woman who likes to wear strong colors or an unusual piece of jewelry. If you are a man, you like it when you dress differently from other men. When others have suits on, you'll wear jeans and a sweater.

The Rabbit
1939 1951 1963 1975 1987 1999
Women usually have lovely hair and like beautiful things. They choose clothes carefully. Men are fussy about dressing and follow the latest trends.

The Dragon
1940 1952 1964 1976 1988 2000
You are the kind of person who likes people to notice you, so you sometimes wear unusual clothes. Also, you often have trouble finding comfortable shoes, so you like to go barefoot.

B Find the year of your birth and sign. What does it say about you? Do you agree? What do you think the signs for these people could be?

1. Steve's friends think he wears strange clothes. His favorite outfit is a bright red jacket with green pants and a purple tie.
   Sign: _____

2. Wanda loves to wear new clothes when she goes out. However, she gets really annoyed when people don't compliment her on what she's wearing.
   Sign: _____

3. Carl is the sort of man who doesn't pay much attention to his clothes, but his hair always looks great. He goes to the best salon in town.
   Sign: _____

4. Stephanie is someone who always wears extremely bright colors. She also usually wears an interesting necklace and earrings.
   Sign: _____

C Do you ever read your horoscope? Do you believe what it says or do you read it just for fun?

That's what friends are for! • 3

6 Match the clauses in column A with the most suitable clauses in column B.

A	B
1. I like it ____	a. when someone criticizes me in front of other people.
2. I don't mind it ____	b. when people are easygoing and friendly.
3. It upsets me ____	c. when rich people are stingy.
4. It embarrasses me ____	d. when people are a few minutes late for an appointment.

7 Write sentences about these situations. Use the expressions in the box.

> I love it . . . I can't stand it . . . I don't like it . . .
> It's so irritating . . . It bothers me . . . I don't mind it . . .
> I really like it . . . It makes me happy . . . It embarrasses me . . .

1. _It's so irritating when someone jumps in front of me in a line._

2. _____

3. _____

4. _____

5. _____

6. _____

4 • Unit 1

8 What are some things you like and don't like about people? Write two sentences about each of the following. Use the ideas in the pictures and your own ideas.

1. What I really like:
   I love it when someone is generous and gives me flowers.
   It makes me happy when _____

2. What I don't like:
   It bothers me when _____

3. What really doesn't bother me:
   I really don't mind it when _____

4. What upsets or embarrasses me:
   It upsets me when _____

That's what friends are for! • 5

9 It really bugs me!

Choose one of the things from Exercise 8 that really embarrasses, bothers, or upsets you. Write two short paragraphs about it. In the first paragraph, describe the situation. In the second paragraph, say why this situation is difficult for you and describe a situation you would prefer.

> It really embarrasses me when someone is too generous to me. Recently, I dated a guy who was always giving me things. For my birthday, he bought me a new CD player, and he treated me to dinner and a movie.
> The problem is, I don't have enough money to treat him in the same way. I'd prefer to date someone I have more in common with. In fact, my ideal boyfriend is someone who is sensible and saves his money!

_____
_____
_____
_____
_____
_____
_____
_____

10 Choose the correct word to complete each sentence.

1. I can tell Simon anything, and I know he won't tell anyone else.
   I can really _____ him to be reliable. (believe / treat / trust)

2. Rita is always criticizing people. She's so _____ – she can never find anything positive to say about anyone. (intolerant / moody / supportive)

3. It bothers me when people are indirect. I prefer people who are _____ . (irritating / rude / straightforward)

4. I like it when someone expresses strong _____ . Hearing other people's views can really make you think. (accomplishments / conversationalists / opinions)

5. Jackie is very rich, but she only spends her money on herself.
   She's very _____ . (generous / modest / stingy)

6 • Unit 1

2 Career moves

1 What's your job?

A Match the jobs with their definitions.

A/An . . .   is a person who . . . .

1. air traffic controller _f_
2. choir director ___
3. counselor ___
4. pharmacist ___
5. veterinarian ___
6. Web designer ___

a. advises people about personal or professional problems
b. creates pages with text and graphics for the Internet
c. conducts or leads a group of singers
d. supplies medicine and advises people about how to take it
e. specializes in giving medical treatment to animals
f. uses a radio to direct the safe movement of airplanes

B Write a definition for each of these jobs: accountant, architect, and fashion designer.

1. _An accountant is someone who_ _____
2. _____
3. _____

2 Challenging or frightening?

A Which words have a positive meaning and which ones have a negative meaning? Write **P** or **N**.

awful _N_   fantasci ___
boring ___   fascinating ___
challenging ___   frightening ___
dangerous ___   interesting ___
difficult ___   rewarding ___

studying ancient cultures

B Write about three jobs you know. Use the words in part A and gerund phrases.

Example: _I think studying ancient cultures, people, and places could be dangerous!_

1. _____
2. _____
3. _____

3 Career choices

A Match each career and the most appropriate job responsibility.

Careers	Job responsibilities
work for an airline	do research
with computers	teach discipline and fitness
as a high school coach	learn new software programs
be a university professor	spend a lot of time alone
a writer	travel to different countries

B Use the information from part A and gerund phrases to complete this conversation.

Ann: So, what kind of career would you like, Tom?

Tom: Well, I'm not exactly sure. *Being a writer* could be interesting. Maybe writing articles for magazines.

Ann: Hmm. I don't know if I'd like that because I'd hate _____ and always being inside.

Tom: What do you want to do, then?

Ann: Well, I'm not sure, either! I'd love _____. I'd really enjoy being with teenagers all day and _____. On the other hand, I'd be interested in _____.

Tom: Really? What would you like about that?

Ann: Well, I'd love _____ all over the world.

Tom: Oh, I could never do it! I think it would be very tiring work.

C Write a short conversation like the one in part B. Use the remaining information in part A or your own ideas.

A: So what kind of career would you like?

B: Well, I'm not exactly sure. _____

A: That sounds interesting. But I wouldn't like it because _____

B: What do you want to do, then?

A: Well, I'd love _____

B: _____

A: _____

8 • Unit 2

4 What a job!

A Read the magazine interviews. Write the correct job title above each interview, and underline the words and phrases that helped you find the answer.

1. _____

All my friends seem to earn more than I do. I suppose it's easier if you have a 9 to 5 job. I work on people's houses and manage construction sites all day. I stay pretty fit doing that, and I enjoy being outside. But in the evenings, I have to make phone calls and do paperwork. It never seems to end!

2. _____

Working for yourself is hard because you are responsible for everything. If no one calls you and asks you to work for them, you have to go out and look for work. Luckily, I now have some regular clients. I paint pictures for some expensive hotels. Right now, I'm doing some paintings for the rooms of a new hotel in Hawaii.

3. _____

My friends say my work is less demanding than theirs, but I work just as hard as they do. I spend a lot of time alone because my job can't begin until all the construction work is completed. Usually, the rooms look great when I've finished my work. Sometimes customers choose really ugly colors, but I have to do what they want.

4. _____

The musicians I lead are extremely talented, and we work together to make sure they sound as good as possible. We often work evenings and weekends, and we travel a lot. Working with a large number of people can be challenging, and it really bothers me if someone is moody because it affects everyone else.

B Which of these jobs would you most enjoy doing? Why?

Career moves • 9

5

First, use words from the list to complete the name of each job title. Then choose the best expressions to compare the jobs in each sentence.

☐ assistant   ☐ instructor   ☑ sitter   ☐ ranger
☐ decorator   ☐ painter   ☐ speaker   ☐ walker

1. A baby- *sitter* _____ doesn't earn *as much as* _____ a teacher.
   ☑ as much as   ☐ greater than   ☐ worse than

2. A chef's _____ has _____ a waiter.
   ☐ as bad hours as   ☐ not as good hours as   ☐ worse hours than

3. A dog _____ is _____ a student intern.
   ☐ more interesting than   ☐ not as boring as   ☐ better paid than

4. A house _____ earns _____ a camp counselor.
   ☐ as bad as   ☐ more than   ☐ not more than

5. A park _____ is _____ a landscaper.
   ☐ as bad as   ☐ not as well paid as   ☐ worse than

6. Being a yoga _____ is _____ being a professor.
   ☐ more than   ☐ as much as   ☐ not as difficult as

7. Being an interior _____ is _____ being a sales assistant.
   ☐ greater than   ☐ earns more than   ☐ more interesting than

8. A public _____ has _____ an office worker.
   ☐ fewer hours than   ☐ not more than   ☐ not as long as

6

Complete these sentences with the correct prepositions.

1. Wai-man works _____ the best Chinese restaurant in Vancouver.
2. I think working _____ other people is more fun than working alone.
3. I would hate working _____ the media. It would be nerve-racking!
4. Working _____ a dance instructor sounds great.
5. Working _____ an office is less interesting than working _____ a cruise ship.

☐ as
☐ at
☐ in
☐ on
☐ with

7 Use the words in parentheses to compare the jobs.

Assistant needed at an outdoor swimming pool. Must be able to swim. Responsible for keeping pool and changing rooms clean. $6/hour. Tues.–Fri. 12–7.

Learn Web design! In search of a bright young person to work as an intern for an advertising agency. Some clerical work. $8/hour. Mon.–Fri. 9–5.

1. A: *An assistant at a swimming pool has shorter hours than an intern.*
   (shorter hours)

   B: *Yes, but working as an intern is more interesting than being a swimming pool assistant.*
   (interesting)

Travel agency needs energetic people. Knowledge of a second language is a plus. Mostly answering the phone. $10/hour. Flexible hours. Three vacation days.

Tutors in math, science, English, and music wanted at private summer school. Challenging work with gifted teenagers. Salary negotiable. Mon.–Sat. 3–7.

2. A: *Working in a* _____
   (better benefits)

   B: *Yes, but working* _____
   (challenging)

Tennis instructor needed at summer camp for 12- and 13-year-olds. Must be excellent tennis player and good with kids. $12/hour. Mon.–Fri. 1–7.

Tour company seeks **guide** to lead bus tours. Great attitude and good speaking voice a must! Fun work, but must be willing to work long hours. $15/hour.

3. A: _____
   (not/much)

   B: _____
   (longer hours)

City seeks **taxi drivers** for morning shift. No experience necessary; driver's license required. $10/hour plus tips. Mon.–Thu. 7 A.M.–2 P.M.

Office assistant required in small, friendly office. Computer skills an advantage. Interesting work. Some management skills necessary. $15/hour. 6-day week.

4. A: _____
   (a shorter work week)

   B: _____
   (less boring)

8

Choose four pairs of jobs to compare. Say which job you would prefer and give two reasons.

- a graphic designer/a TV news director
- an architect/a teacher
- a doctor/a dentist
- a conductor/a musician
- a gardener/a landscaper
- a typist/a Web designer
- working on a construction site/ working in an office
- being self-employed/working for a company

Example: *Working as a TV news director sounds more interesting than being a graphic designer. A TV news director has more responsibility than a graphic designer. Also, directing the news is better paid.*

1. _____

2. _____

3. _____

4. _____

3 Could you do me a favor?

1 Would you mind . . . ?

A Complete the request for each situation.

1. You want to borrow a dollar from a friend for a cup of coffee.
   <u>Can I borrow a dollar for a cup of coffee?</u>

2. You want a classmate to give you a ride home after class.
   <u>Would you mind</u>

3. You want to turn down your roommate's TV.
   <u>Is it OK if</u>

4. You want to use a friend's cell phone.
   <u>Do you mind if</u>

5. You want to borrow a friend's car for the weekend.
   <u>Would it be OK if</u>

6. You want someone to tell you how to get to the subway.
   <u>I was wondering if</u>

B Think of four things you would need to have done if you were going on a long vacation. Write requests asking a friend to do the things.

Example: <u>Could you water the plants?</u>

1.
2.
3.
4.

2

Accept or decline these requests. For requests you decline, give excuses. Use the expressions in the box or expressions of your own.

Accepting	Declining
That's OK, I guess.	Sorry, but . . .
I'd be glad to.	I'd like to, but . . .
Fine. No problem.	

1. A: Can I use your computer? I have to type a paper.
   B: <u>Sorry, but I'm going to use it myself in a few minutes.</u>

2. A: I've just finished this ten-page paper. Could you check it for me, please?
   B: _____

3. A: I wonder if I could stay at your place for a week while my landlord fixes the roof.
   B: _____

4. A: Would you mind if I used your cell phone to make a long-distance call to Nigeria?
   B: _____

3

Look at the pictures and write the conversations. Speaker A makes a request. Speaker B declines it. Each speaker should give a reason.

1. A: <u>I was wondering if you'd mind carrying these suitcases for me. I have a bad back.</u>
   B: <u>Sorry, but I have a bad back, too.</u>

2. A: _____
   B: _____

3. A: _____
   B: _____

14 • Unit 3

4 Getting what you want

A Read the magazine article about making requests.

Requests that get RESULTS

There are many different ways of making requests. For example, if someone wants to borrow a dollar, he or she can say:

"Could you lend me a dollar?"
"Do you have a dollar?"
"You don't have a dollar, do you?"

How does a person know which request to use? Language researchers have suggested that speakers must make several important decisions. First, they must consider the other person's feelings because requests can sometimes cause embarrassment to both the speaker and the listener. If the speaker thinks the listener will accept the request, he or she will probably use a less formal request; however, if the speaker thinks the listener may decline the request, he or she will probably use a fairly formal request. The listener then has to make a choice either to accept or refuse the request. If he or she refuses, then both the speaker and the listener might be embarrassed.

In addition, speakers must decide how well they know the person they are requesting something from and choose a suitable question. If the speaker knows the listener well, one of several types of requests can be used.

For example:
1. Make a statement with *need*: "I need a dollar."
2. Use an imperative: "Please lend me a dollar."
3. Use a question: "Do you have a dollar?"

If the speaker doesn't know the listener well, one of several types of requests can be used instead. For example:
4. Ask about ability: "Could/Can you lend me a dollar?"
5. Be polite – use *may*: "May I borrow a dollar?"
6. Ask for permission: "Would it be OK if I borrowed a dollar?"
7. Express curiosity: "I wonder if I could borrow a dollar."
8. State the request negatively: "I don't suppose you could lend me a dollar."
9. Apologize: "I hope you don't mind my asking you for a dollar?"
10. Give a hint: "I wish I had a dollar."

Knowing how to make requests means knowing different types of requests as well as when each type of request is appropriate.

B Check (✓) if each request is less formal or more formal. Then write the correct number from the article (1–10) for each type of request.

	Less formal	More formal	Type
1. Close the door.	☐	☐	___
2. It's really cold in here.	☐	☐	___
3. Could you possibly move your car?	☐	☐	___
4. May I borrow your dictionary?	☐	☐	___
5. I wonder if you could help me with this assignment.	☐	☐	___
6. I need some help moving to my new apartment.	☐	☐	___

C When do you usually use each type of request? Which of the ten types of requests described in the article do you use most often? least often?

5 Nouns and verbs

A Complete this chart. Then check your answers in a dictionary.

Noun	Verb	Noun	Verb
apology	*apologize*	invitation	_____
compliment	_____	permission	_____
explanation	_____	request	_____

B Check (✓) the phrase that describes what each person is doing.

I really like your new haircut.

1. I really like your new haircut.
   ☐ giving a reason
   ☐ giving a compliment

2. Don't worry, I know you didn't mean to break it.
   ☐ returning a favor
   ☐ accepting an apology

3. Can I borrow your laptop?
   ☐ asking for a favor
   ☐ giving a gift

4. I can't lend you my bike because I need it myself.
   ☐ denying a request
   ☐ accepting an invitation

5. I was wondering if you'd mind helping me cook dinner.
   ☐ making a request
   ☐ returning a compliment

6 Choose the correct words.

1. My phone didn't work for a week. The phone company _____ an apology and took $20 off my bill.
   (accepted / denied / offered)

2. A friend of mine really loves to _____ compliments, but he never gives anyone else one. I don't understand why he's like that.
   (do / owe / receive)

3. Carol is always talking on the phone. She makes a lot of calls, but she rarely _____ mine. Maybe she never listens to her voice mail!
   (makes / offers / returns)

4. I need to _____ a favor. Could you please give me a ride to school tomorrow? My bike has a flat tire!
   (ask for / give / turn down)

7 Use these messages to complete the phone conversations. Use indirect requests.

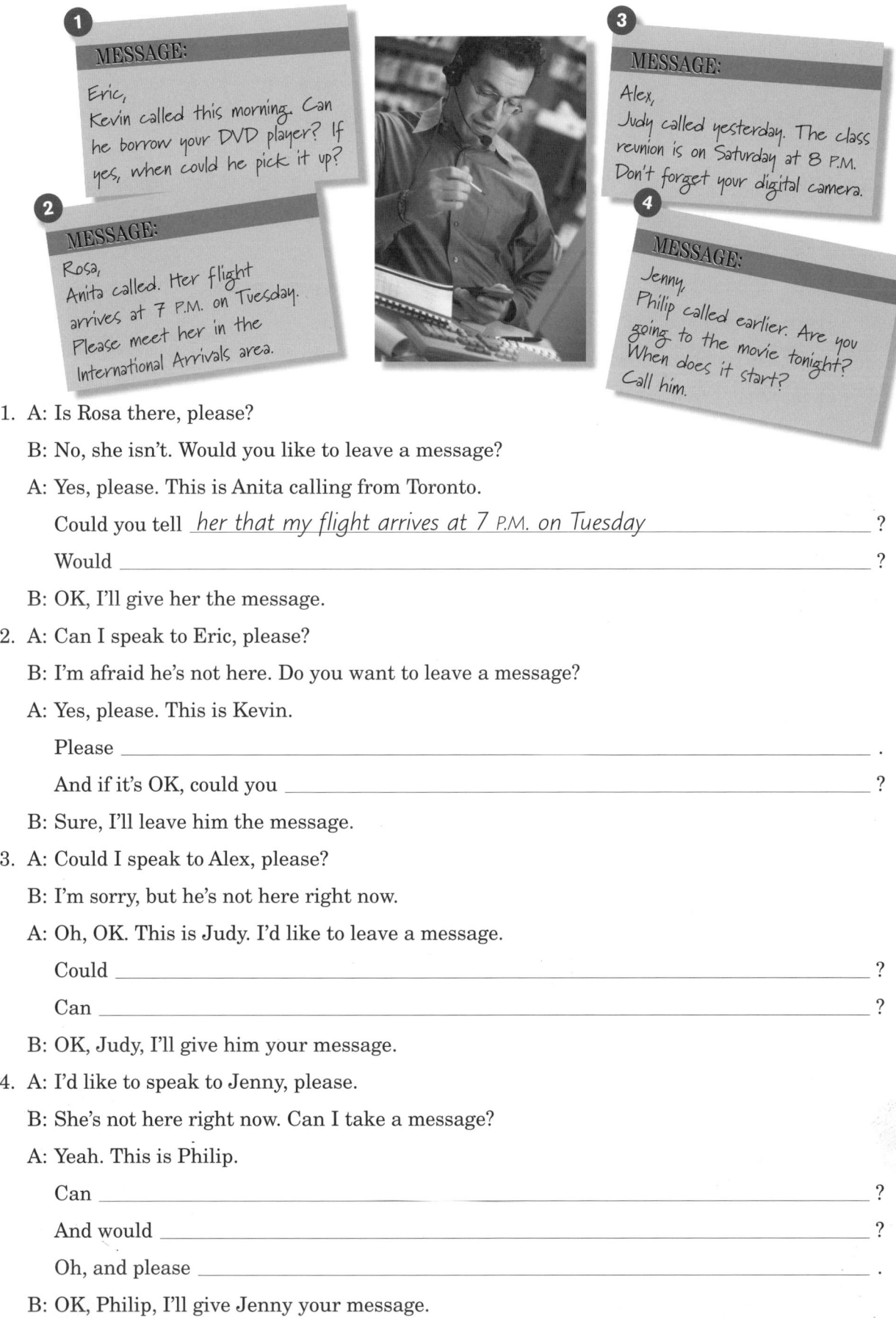

1
MESSAGE:
Eric,
Kevin called this morning. Can he borrow your DVD player? If yes, when could he pick it up?

2
MESSAGE:
Rosa,
Anita called. Her flight arrives at 7 P.M. on Tuesday. Please meet her in the International Arrivals area.

3
MESSAGE:
Alex,
Judy called yesterday. The class reunion is on Saturday at 8 P.M. Don't forget your digital camera.

4
MESSAGE:
Jenny,
Philip called earlier. Are you going to the movie tonight? When does it start? Call him.

1. A: Is Rosa there, please?

   B: No, she isn't. Would you like to leave a message?

   A: Yes, please. This is Anita calling from Toronto.

   Could you tell _her that my flight arrives at 7 P.M. on Tuesday_ ?

   Would _____ ?

   B: OK, I'll give her the message.

2. A: Can I speak to Eric, please?

   B: I'm afraid he's not here. Do you want to leave a message?

   A: Yes, please. This is Kevin.

   Please _____ .

   And if it's OK, could you _____ ?

   B: Sure, I'll leave him the message.

3. A: Could I speak to Alex, please?

   B: I'm sorry, but he's not here right now.

   A: Oh, OK. This is Judy. I'd like to leave a message.

   Could _____ ?

   Can _____ ?

   B: OK, Judy, I'll give him your message.

4. A: I'd like to speak to Jenny, please.

   B: She's not here right now. Can I take a message?

   A: Yeah. This is Philip.

   Can _____ ?

   And would _____ ?

   Oh, and please _____ .

   B: OK, Philip, I'll give Jenny your message.

Could you do me a favor? • 17

8 Complete the conversation with the information in the box. Add any words necessary and use the correct form of the verbs given.

- ☐ ask Jill to get some soda
- ☐ borrow some money
- ☑ borrow your CD player
- ☐ bring a big salad
- ☐ can buy dessert
- ☐ don't be late

Chris: So, is there anything I can do to help?

Len: Yeah. Would it be OK _if I borrowed your CD player_ ? We need good stereo sound at the party.

Chris: Sure. And I'll bring some CDs. I have some great party music.

Len: Thanks.

Chris: No problem. Now, what about food?

Len: Well, I thought maybe a salad. Would you mind _____ , too?

Chris: Well, OK. And, how about drinks?

Len: Well, I was also wondering if you'd mind _____ .

And please tell her _____ .

Last time we had a party, she didn't arrive till eleven o'clock, and everyone got really thirsty!

Chris: I remember.

Len: One more thing, I wonder if you _____ .

Chris: Um, sure. All right. But, uh, would you mind if I _____ to pay for it?

9 Rewrite these sentences. Find another way to say each sentence using the words given.

1. Can I use your cell phone?
   Would it be OK if I used your cell phone? (OK)

2. Please ask Penny to stop by and talk to me.
   _____ (would)

3. Could I borrow your guitar?
   _____ (wonder)

4. Would you ask Adam what time he's coming over?
   _____ (could / when)

5. Lend me your hairbrush.
   _____ (mind)

18 • Unit 3

4 What a story!

1 Complete these news stories using the verbs from the list.

☑ carrying   ☐ had   ☐ missed   ☐ said
☐ disappearing   ☐ happened   ☐ reported

1.

Aircraft in Near Collision

On Tuesday, a jumbo jet that was _carrying_ 382 passengers and an Air Force plane _____ each other by 15 meters in mid-air over the Atlantic Ocean. A spokesperson for the airline company, which _____ the near miss in a statement yesterday, said the incident _____ so quickly that neither pilot _____ time to take evasive action. "There was no warning whatsoever," _____ the captain of the jumbo jet. He looked out of the window and saw the tail of the Air Force plane as it was _____ into the clouds.

☐ felt   ☐ got   ☐ passing   ☐ said   ☐ turned
☐ gave   ☐ jogging   ☐ realized   ☐ thought

2.

JOGGER GETS A SHOCK

A jogger _____ the shock of his life when he was _____ around a city park on Saturday. "As I was _____ under a large tree, I _____ something drop on me," he recalled. "At first, I _____ it was a branch, but then I _____ it was a snake! I couldn't believe it! Then the guy running ahead of me _____ around and saw it slide off. The snake wasn't particularly big, but it _____ me quite a shock all the same." A snake expert _____ the snake was probably a python, which is non-poisonous.

19

2

Join each sentence in column A with an appropriate sentence in column B. Use as, when, or while to join the sentences.

A	B
I was crossing the road.	My racquet broke.
I was using my computer.	A car nearly hit me.
We were playing tennis.	The water went cold.
I was taking a shower.	I burned my finger.
I was cooking dinner.	It suddenly stopped working.

1. *As I was crossing the road, a car nearly hit me.*
2. _____
3. _____
4. _____
5. _____

3

Complete these conversations. Use the past tense or the past continuous of the verbs given.

1. A: I'm sorry I'm so late, Kathy. I was at the dentist.

   B: Don't tell me! While you <u>were sitting</u> (sit) in the waiting room, you _____ (meet) someone interesting. I know how you are, Tom!

   A: Well, you're wrong this time. The dentist _____ (clean) my teeth when she suddenly _____ (get) called away for an emergency. So I just sat there waiting for two hours with my mouth hanging open!

2. A: Guess what happened to me last night! As I _____ (get) into bed, I _____ (hear) a loud noise like a gunshot in the street. Then the phone _____ (ring).

   B: Who was it?

   A: It was Mariana. She always calls me late at night, but this time she had a reason. She _____ (drive) right past my apartment when she _____ (get) a flat tire. It was very late, so while we _____ (change) the tire, I _____ (invite) her to spend the night.

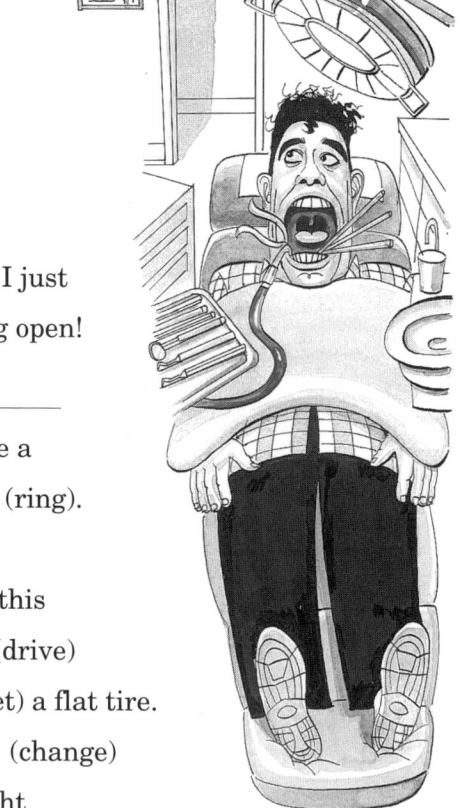

20 • Unit 4

4 Lost and found

A Read this newspaper story.

Fishermen found safe and sound

Three Taiwanese fishermen were rescued yesterday from a small uninhabited island in the South Pacific. The men had disappeared for more than three months.

They had left Taiwan in a small fishing boat and had planned a week-long trip. On their fifth day, however, they encountered a typhoon, and it badly damaged their boat. Fortunately, no one was hurt. After the storm had passed, though, they discovered that the engine wouldn't start, so their boat just drifted at sea for over a month. During this time, the fishermen caught fish to eat and drank rain water to stay alive.

Finally, the boat drifted toward a small island. When it got close enough, the men jumped out and swam to shore. On the island, they found fresh fruit and vegetables, and they continued to catch fish to eat.

The fishermen had lived on the island for two months when a passing ship rescued them. Although the three men had lost a lot of weight, they were still in fairly good shape. Their families feared that the fishermen had died during the typhoon. They were surprised and happy that the ship had found them and that they were safe and sound.

B Answer these questions.

1. How long were the fishermen missing?

2. How long had they planned to be away?

3. What happened to the boat in the storm?

4. What did they do to stay alive?

5. How were they rescued?

C What do you think the fishermen did all day on the boat for a month? for two months on the island? What would you do?

What a story! • 21

5

Imagine you got lost like the men in Exercise 4. Write two paragraphs. In the first paragraph, describe how you got lost. In the second, say how you got home.

Where were you when you got lost?
What were you doing?
How long were you lost?
How did you find your way back?
Were you rescued? How?

_____
_____
_____
_____
_____

> A couple of years ago, I got lost in the mountains. I was hiking when it suddenly got foggy. I was really frightened because I couldn't see anything, and it was getting cold. I decided to put up my tent and stay there for the night.
> While I was putting up my tent, though, the fog began to clear. . . .

6

Choose the correct verbs to complete the story.

Grammar note: After

In sentences using **after** that show one past event occurring before another, the clause with **after** usually uses the past perfect.

After the storm **had passed**, they discovered that the engine wouldn't start.

Bob and I ____had just gotten____ engaged, so we
(just got / had just gotten)

went to a jewelry store to buy a wedding ring. We _____ a ring when a
(just chose / had just chosen)

man with a gun _____ . After the robber _____ Bob's
(came in / had come in)   (took / had taken)

wallet, he _____ the ring. I _____ it to him when the
(demanded / had demanded)   (just handed / had just handed)

alarm _____ to go off, and the robber _____ . We were
(started / had started)   (ran off / had run off)

so relieved! But then the sales assistant _____ us we had to pay for the ring
(told / had told)

because I _____ it to the robber. We _____ her
(gave / had given)   (just told / had just told)

that we wouldn't pay for it when the police _____ and
(arrived / had arrived)

_____ us! What a terrible experience!
(arrested / had arrested)

22 • Unit 4

7 What a story!

A Choose the best headline for each of these news stories.

> **What a disaster!**
> **What a predicament!**
> **What an emergency!**
> **What a triumph!**
> **What a lucky break!**

1. _____
Joan Smith was seven months pregnant when she and her husband, Hank, went on vacation to a small, **remote** island off the coast of South America. The first night, Joan was in a lot of pain. There were no doctors on the island, and the hotel where they were staying didn't even have a phone. Hank had almost given up when he finally found the only phone on the island. He called a hospital on the **mainland**, and half an hour later a helicopter picked Joan up and took her to the hospital – just in time for her to have a beautiful baby girl.

2. _____
Victoria Peters was very sick for several months before her final exams this summer. She simply couldn't study at all. Her parents suggested she should **skip** a year and take the exams the next summer. **Remarkably**, Victoria got well suddenly just before the exams, spent the next two weeks studying, and got the highest grade in her class!

3. _____
Jesse Peterson had waited years for a **promotion**. Finally, a week ago, he was offered the position he had always wanted – Regional Manager. On the same day, however, he won $6 million in the lottery. Jesse's wife wants him to **resign** from his job and take her on a trip around the world. Jesse says he cannot decide what to do.

B Look at the words in **bold**. What you think they mean?

remote _____   skip _____   promotion _____

mainland _____   remarkably _____   resign _____

8

Complete the sentences. Use the simple past, the past continuous, or the past perfect of the verbs given.

1. After an art show _____*opened*_____ (open) in New York, it was discovered that someone _____ (hang) a famous painting by Henri Matisse upside-down.

2. In 1960, a Turkish diver _____ (discover) the remains of a 3,000-year-old shipwreck while he _____ (dive) for sponges off the coast of southwest Turkey.

3. A big earthquake _____ (strike) central Taiwan in 1999. Such a dangerous earthquake _____ (not strike) the area for many years.

4. In 2003, Italian workers _____ (find) important archaeological remains while they _____ (construct) a new parking lot in Vatican City. There were mosaics dating from A.D. 54–68.

9 *Read this situation. Then use the information and clues to complete the chart. Write the name of each reporter and each country. (You will leave one square in the chart blank.)*

Ms. Anderson   Ms. Benson   Mr. Jackson   Mr. Marks   Mr. Swire

Five news reporters – two women and three men – arrived for an international conference on Sunday, Monday, and Tuesday. No more than two people came on the same day. The reporters came from five different countries.

Clues
The women: Ms. Anderson and Ms. Benson
The men: Mr. Jackson, Mr. Marks, and Mr. Swire
The countries: Australia, Canada, Italy, Singapore, and the United States

The arrivals:
- Mr. Swire arrived late at night. No one else had arrived that day.
- Ms. Anderson and Mr. Marks arrived on the same day. The man from Singapore had arrived the day before.
- The reporters from Italy and Australia arrived on the same day.
- Mr. Jackson and the woman from Italy arrived on Tuesday, after Mr. Marks.
- The reporter from Australia had arrived the day after the person from the United States.
- Mr. Marks is from North America but not the United States.

Reporters' countries and arrival days		
Sunday	Name: _____ Country: _____	Name: _____ Country: _____
Monday	Name: _____ Country: _____	Name: _____ Country: _____
Tuesday	Name: _____ Country: _____	Name: _____ Country: _____

5 Crossing cultures

1 **Complete these sentences. Use words from the list.**

☐ confident   ☐ depressed   ☑ embarrassed   ☐ fascinated   ☐ uncomfortable

1. In my country, people never leave tips. So when I first went abroad, I kept forgetting to tip waiters. I felt really _embarrassed_ .

2. The first time I traveled abroad, I felt really _____ . I was alone, I didn't speak the language, and I didn't make any friends.

3. I just spent a year in France learning to speak French. It was a satisfying experience, and I was _____ by the culture.

4. At first I really didn't like shopping in the open-air markets. I felt _____ because so many people were trying to sell me something at the same time.

5. When I arrived in Lisbon, I was nervous because I couldn't speak any Portuguese. As I began to learn the language, though, I became more _____ about living there.

2 **Respond to the questions about traveling. Write complete sentences using** one thing, the (only) thing, *or* something.

1. Would you be nervous about being far away from your family?
   One thing I'd be nervous about is being far away from my family. OR
   Being far away from my family is something I'd be comfortable with.

2. Would you feel insecure about traveling alone?
   _____

3. Would you be enthusiastic about making new friends?
   _____

4. Would you be curious about the way people live in other places?
   _____

5. Would you be anxious about spending too much money?
   _____

25

3 I'd be anxious . . .

A Imagine you are going to travel to a country you have never visited before. Write sentences using the factors and feelings given. Then add another sentence explaining your feelings.

Factors	Feelings
public transportation	anxious (about)
the architecture	comfortable (with)
the climate	curious (about)
the food	enthusiastic (about)
the language	fascinated (by)
the money	nervous (about)
the music	uncertain (about)
the people my age	uncomfortable (with)
	worried (about)

Example:
Public transportation is something I'd be anxious about.
I'd be afraid of getting lost.

1.
2.
3.
4.
5.
6.
7.
8.

B Are most of your feelings about traveling to a foreign country positive or negative? Why?

26 • Unit 5

4 Culture shock!

A What two main differences have you noticed between your own culture and another one?

B Read this article from a student travel Web site. Does the article make you think of any other differences?

Each society has its own beliefs, attitudes, customs, behaviors, and social habits. These give people a sense of who they are, how they are supposed to behave, and what they should or should not do.

People become conscious of such rules when they meet people from different cultures. For example, the rules about when to eat vary from culture to culture. Many North Americans and Europeans organize their timetables around three mealtimes a day. In other countries, on the other hand, it's not the custom to have strict rules like this – people eat when they want to, and every family has its own timetable.

When people visit or live in a country for the first time, they are often surprised at the differences that exist between their own culture and the culture in the other country. For some people, traveling abroad is the thing they enjoy most in life; for others, though, cultural differences make them feel uncomfortable, frightened, or even insecure. This is known as "culture shock."

When you're visiting a foreign country, it is important to understand and appreciate cultural differences. This can help people avoid misunderstandings, develop friendships more easily, and feel more comfortable when traveling or living abroad.

Here are several things to do in order to avoid culture shock.

1. Avoid quick judgments; try to understand people in another culture from their own point of view.
2. Become aware of what is going on around you, and why.
3. Don't think of your cultural habits as "right" and other people's as "wrong."
4. Be willing to try new things and to have new experiences.
5. Try to appreciate and understand other people's values.
6. Think about your own culture and how it influences your attitudes and actions.
7. Avoid having negative stereotypes about foreigners and cultures.
8. Show interest in as well as respect, sincerity, acceptance, and concern for things that are important to other people.

C Use your own words to write definitions for these words.

1. culture _____
2. culture shock _____
3. stereotypes _____

D Choose two pieces of advice in the reading that you think are the most important for avoiding culture shock. Why do you think they are especially important?

Advice	Why it is important

Crossing cultures

5 Complete these sentences giving information about customs in a country you know.

1. If you go for a long ride in a friend's car,
   <u>it's the custom to offer to pay some of the expenses.</u>

2. When a friend graduates from school or college, _____

3. If you borrow something from a friend, _____

4. When a friend invites you to dinner, _____

6 Contrasting customs

A Read the information about the different customs and find four pairs of countries with contrasting customs. Write the countries in the blanks below.

Country	Custom
Brazil	Friends kiss each other three or four times on the cheeks as a greeting.
Denmark	People generally arrive on time for most occasions.
Egypt	People allow their hosts to treat them to meals in restaurants.
France	Service is usually included in the price of a meal in restaurants.
Japan	People bow when they see or meet someone they know.
New Zealand	People usually pay for their own meals in restaurants.
Spain	People usually arrive late for most appointments.
United States	People leave a tip of 15–20 percent in restaurants.

1. <u>Brazil and Japan</u>   3. _____
2. _____   4. _____

28 • Unit 5

B Read these six cross-cultural situations. Write sentences describing what the visitors did wrong. Use the expressions in the box.

> you're (not) supposed to
> you're (not) expected to
> it's (not) the custom to
> it's (not) acceptable to

1. Hanne is from Denmark. When she was on vacation in Spain, some Spanish friends invited her to dinner at 9:00. She arrived at exactly 9:00, but her friends had not even arrived home yet.
   In Spain, you're expected to _____

2. Marylou is from the United States. During her first week in Paris, she went to a restaurant with some new friends. She was so happy with the service that she left a tip of 20 percent. Her friends were really embarrassed.
   In France, _____

3. Peter is from New Zealand. When he went to Egypt, he was invited to dinner at a restaurant. When the bill came, he offered to pay for his dinner. His Egyptian friend was pretty upset.
   In Egypt, _____

4. Susana is from Brazil. She was working for a year in Osaka, Japan. One day, when she saw a Japanese co-worker in a bookstore, she went to say hello and kissed him on the cheeks. Her friend was shocked and embarrassed and left the store quickly.

5. Adam is from Canada. He was on vacation in Bali, Indonesia, and some new friends invited him to a temple to watch a special dance performance. He arrived on time wearing a clean T-shirt and shorts, but they said he couldn't go inside the temple because he wasn't dressed properly.

Crossing cultures • 29

7

What advice would you give travelers with these problems and worries? Use the expressions in the box.

> One thing to remember is . . .
> Something to keep in mind is . . .
> One thing visitors often don't realize is . . .
> Something to consider is . . .

1. A: I'd really miss my family.
   B: <u>One thing to remember is that international phone calls are usually cheaper on weekends.</u>

2. A: I often get a stomachache when I go abroad.
   B: _____

3. A: I'd feel nervous about carrying lots of cash around with me.
   B: _____

4. A: I think I'd get suspicious about the prices of some things.
   B: _____

5. A: I wouldn't be very sure of myself.
   B: _____

8

Write about living in a foreign country. In the first two paragraphs, write about two things you would enjoy and two things you might worry about. In the third paragraph, write about the country's customs.

> If I lived in Colombia, I'd enjoy learning about the music scene — the local bands and singers who are popular there. Another thing I'd be fascinated by is . . .
> However, one thing that I'd be nervous about is . . .
> I've heard that when you visit someone, it's the custom to . . .

30 • Unit 5

6 What's wrong with it?

1 **A** What can be wrong with these things? Put these words in the correct categories. (Most words go in more than one category.)

| blouse | car | carpet | chair | mug | pitcher | plate | sink | window |

chipped	cracked	dented	leaking	scratched	stained	torn

B What is wrong with these things? Use the words in part A to write a sentence about each one.

1. _The car is scratched._   OR   2. _____   3. _____
   There's a scratch on the car.

4. _____   5. _____   6. _____

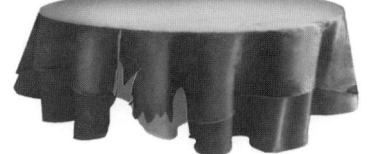
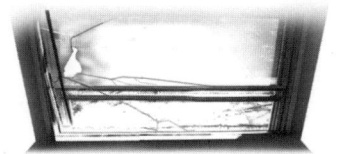

7. _____   8. _____   9. _____

31

2 Problems, problems, problems!

A Have you ever bought something that didn't work right? What did you do about it?
Have you ever had a problem getting a refund? What happened?

B Read about these problems described in *Consumer* magazine.

Consumer Magazine

Sharon's laptops

Sharon Kurtz is a freelance writer who works at home. She bought a laptop from Star Superstore, a discount computer center. When she took it home, she discovered that the screen was fuzzy. The store agreed to exchange it. When a new laptop was delivered to her home, Sharon found that the outside cover was scratched. Again, she complained, so the store offered her a third computer, but this one didn't work right, either. Some of the keys on the keyboard were loose. She was offered a fourth laptop, but it crashed a week after she started using it.

At this point, Sharon got angry and contacted *Consumer* magazine. We wrote Star Superstore a letter explaining that Sharon was losing work because of all the computer problems. The store offered Sharon a full refund plus $1,000 for all the inconvenience she had suffered.

Chris's car

Chris Hill thought his troubles were over when the police found his stolen car, but in fact his problems were only just beginning. The engine was badly damaged, and it needed to be replaced at a cost of $2,300. In addition, the locks were broken, and they needed to be repaired at a cost of $400. Chris's insurance company told him that he would have to pay 40 percent of the cost of the new engine ($920). They argued that the new engine would add 40 percent to the value of his car. However, Chris did not believe this.

Chris knew that the value of a used car depends mainly on its age, so he contacted *Consumer* magazine. One of our lawyers asked the insurance company to prove that the new engine would increase the value of the car. When the insurance company replied, they said they no longer wanted Chris to pay any of the repair costs.

C Complete the chart.

| | Problems | What *Consumer* magazine did | Compensated? |
			Yes	No
1. Sharon's laptops	*fuzzy screen*		☐	☐
2. Chris's car			☐	☐

D What would you have done if you were Sharon? Chris?
Would you have done the same things?

3 Sharpen your skills!

A Choose appropriate verbs to complete the sentences.
Use passive infinitives (*to be* + past participle) or gerunds.

> **Language note: Verbs ending in -en or -n**
>
> Some verbs are formed by adding *-en* or *-n* to a noun or adjective.
> These verbs mean "to make more of something."
>
> | Noun | Verb | Adjective | Verb |
> |---|---|---|---|
> | length | → length**en** | loose | → loos**en** |
> | (make something longer) | | (make something looser) | |

☑ lengthen ☑ loosen ☐ sharpen ☐ straighten ☑ tighten ☐ widen

1. This jacket is too short.
   It needs _to be lengthened_. OR
   It needs _lengthening_.

2. The screws on these glasses are too loose.
   They need _to be tightened_.

3. The blades on these scissors are too dull.
   They need _to be sharpened_.

4. This faucet is too tight.
   It needs _to be loosening_.

5. This road has too many dangerous turns.
   It needs _straightening_.

6. This street is too narrow.
   It needs _to be widened_.

B Can you think of three other verbs ending in *-en* or *-n*?

_____ _____ _____

What's wrong with it? • 33

4

Complete the conversation. Use keep, keeps, need, or needs with passive infinitives or gerunds of the verbs given.

Tim: Guess what? Someone broke into my car last night!

Jan: Oh, no. What did they take?

Tim: Nothing! But they did a lot of damage. The lock <u>needs to be repaired</u>. (repair) And the windows _____. (replace)

Jan: What about your CD player?

Tim: It _____ (turn) on and off. They broke the button. It just _____. (replace)

Jan: It was probably some young kids having "fun."

Tim: Yeah, some fun. I think they had a party in my car! The seats _____. (clean)

Jan: How annoying. Does the car drive OK?

Tim: No, it feels strange. The gears _____ (stick), so they _____. (fix) And the brakes _____ (check) right away.

Jan: Well, I guess you're lucky they didn't steal it!

Tim: Yeah, lucky me.

5

Write about something you bought that had something wrong with it. In the first paragraph, describe the problem. In the second paragraph, explain what you did about it.

> Recently, I bought an espresso machine. While I was unpacking it, I could see it was already damaged. The glass carafe was chipped and needed to be replaced. And to make matters worse, the machine leaked!
>
> I took it back to the store. I was worried because the machine had been on sale, and I had lost my receipt. Luckily, the clerk didn't ask me for it. She said a lot of customers had recently had the same problem, and she gave me a better machine at the same price.

34 • Unit 6

6 Jack will fix it!

A Match each problem with the repair needed.

JACK'S REPAIR SHOP

Item	Problem	Repair needed
1. dishwasher	doesn't work _f_	a. tighten and glue the legs
2. DVD player	DVD is stuck ___	b. repair the wire
3. speakers	wire is damaged ___	c. remove the DVD
4. TV	screen is cracked ___	d. repaint the door
5. stove	metal door is scratched ___	e. replace the screen
6. table	legs are loose ___	✓ f. check the motor

B Write a sentence describing each problem. Then add a sentence describing the action needed to fix it. Use passive infinitives or gerunds.

1. _The dishwasher doesn't work. The motor needs to be checked._ OR _The motor needs checking._

2. _____

3. _____

4. _____

5. _____

6. _____

C Think of three items you own that are damaged (or were damaged) in some way. Write a sentence describing each problem. Then write another sentence describing the action needed to fix it.

1. _____

2. _____

3. _____

What's wrong with it? • 35

7 Complete the crossword puzzle.

Across

1 Do you have another **base** for these flowers? This one is cracked.
4 You can't wear this _____ to your job interview, Dave. Two buttons have come off the front, and the lining is torn.
8 This is a great new food _____. It really helps me chop vegetables more quickly.
10 The buttons on this shirt are _____. They'll come off if they aren't fixed soon.
11 My new dress is _____. I spilled coffee on it.
12 These socks have a hole in them. I'd like to _____ them for another pair, please.
13 The glass in that window is _____. It needs replacing.

Down

2 This carpet is really dirty. It needs to be _____.
3 The _____ beside your desk needs to be emptied. It's full of paper.
5 There's a _____ in your jeans. Look, the left leg is badly torn.
6 I prefer to cook on a gas _____ than to cook on an electric one.
7 The back of my car is slightly _____. Someone drove into it.
9 My car door is _____, and it needs repainting. It looks like someone damaged it with a key.
10 Look! There's a stain on the _____ of your jacket – just inside the collar.

36 • Unit 6

7 The world we live in

1 Use the information in the pamphlet and the verbs and prepositions given below to change the sentences from the active to the passive.

Here are just some of the dangers facing you and your children.

The water we drink
1. Too many dead fish in the rivers are contaminating the water supply.
2. Chlorine and other additives have ruined the taste of our drinking water.

The food we eat
3. The spraying of agricultural pesticides has caused mysterious new illnesses.
4. Pollution from cars and trucks is destroying our crops of fruit and vegetables.

The air we breathe
5. Factory chimneys are releasing extremely dangerous chemicals.
6. Breathing smog every day has damaged many people's health.

The world we live in
7. The lack of rainfall has created more droughts and bigger deserts.
8. Global warming is harming forests and wildlife.

Join Save Our Planet Today

1. <u>Our drinking water is being polluted by dead fish in the rivers.</u> (by)
2. _____ (due to)
3. _____ (by)
4. _____ (because of)
5. _____ (by)
6. _____ (as a result of)
7. _____ (because of)
8. _____ (through)

37

2 Verbs and nouns

A Complete the chart.

Verb	Noun	Verb	Noun
contaminate	contamination	educate	_____
contribute	_____	_____	pollution
_____	creation	protect	_____
deplete	_____	_____	reduction
_____	destruction	threaten	_____

B Write four sentences like the ones in Exercise 1 using words from the chart.

Example: _Many rivers and streams have been badly contaminated by industrial waste._

1. _____
2. _____
3. _____
4. _____

3 Choose the correct words or phrases.

1. Green organizations are trying to save rain forests that have been _____threatened_____ by developers and farmers. (created / ruined / threatened)

2. One way to inform the public about factories that pollute the environment is through _____ programs on TV. (agricultural / educational / industrial)

3. The ozone layer has been _____ more in the southern hemisphere than in the northern hemisphere. (created / destroyed / polluted)

4. Agricultural sprays are _____ the soil in many countries. (damaging / eating up / lowering)

5. _____ is an enormous problem in many large cities where whole families can only afford to live in one room. (pollution / poverty / waste)

El Yunque rain forest

38 • Unit 7

4 How safe are your plastic cards?

A How many of these cards do you have: credit card, store card, ID card, debit card, phone card, library card? How many of them are made of plastic?

B Read the magazine article about plastic cards.

It's in the cards.

Nowadays, many people pay for many things with credit cards. There are now hundreds of millions of credit cards worldwide, but plastic cards don't stop there. Bills and coins are gradually being replaced by "plastic money." Banks are issuing debit cards, and charge cards are being offered by many types of stores and businesses. In many places, people are now using plastic cards at public phones, in the subways, at gas stations, and in supermarkets. In addition, cards that used to be made of paper are being replaced by plastic ones. For example, many gym membership cards are now made of plastic.

How safe is the plastic used to make these cards? Until recently, most cards have been made from a plastic called polyvinyl chloride (PVC). While PVC is being produced, harmful chemicals are released into the atmosphere. One of the most dangerous chemicals released is dioxin, which is known to cause cancer in humans. Another problem is, when a PVC card is thrown away, it is not biodegradable – it does not "break down" and cannot be recycled.

Now there is an alternative to PVC cards. Greenpeace, the environmental organization and charity, has developed an "Earth-friendly" credit card. Their card is composed of a biodegradable plastic that is made with a plant-based material. The card breaks down in around three months in a special soil called compost – in this way, it is completely recycled. By contrast, a PVC card lasts for centuries. Greenpeace hopes that many organizations will follow its example and issue cards that do not pollute the environment.

The World Wildlife Fund (WWF) is one organization that has followed Greenpeace's lead. The WWF's advertising campaign for a "green" credit card states: "If money makes the world go around, you can now help make our world a little greener by taking out the new PVC-free WWF Visa Card." Think what a difference it would make worldwide if all the major banks and credit card companies adopted this safer, more environmentally friendly way to do business!

C Check (✓) the true statements. For statements that are false, write the true information.

1. ☐ Many different types of cards today are made of plastic.

2. ☐ The plastic used in making most credit cards is fairly safe.

3. ☐ The biodegradable Greenpeace credit card is not made of plastic.

4. ☐ WWF's attempt to get rid of toxic chemicals is supported by their new PVC-free Visa card.

5. ☐ Now all banks and credit card companies offer PVC-free credit cards to their customers.

D Do you have any plastic cards? Did you know that they are not recyclable? Do you have (or want to get) a PVC-free or "green" card?

5 Nouns beginning with over

A Match the nouns and definitions.

Nouns
1. overbuilding ___e___
2. overcrowding ___f___
3. overflowing ___d___
4. overpopulation ___b___
5. overuse ___a___
6. overburdened ___c___

Definitions
a. put something to a particular purpose too often
b. too many people for a limited amount of food, housing, and materials available for them to live there
c. having too much of something to deal with
d. having too many people or things to be contained; spilling over
e. too many structures and homes in a certain area
f. too many people or things in a restricted area

B Choose the correct noun from part A to complete each sentence.

1. Although ___overpopulation___ is a major world problem, overall birth rates are beginning to slow as women choose to have fewer children, and at an older age.
2. In some major cities, the problem of ___overbuilding___ is a result of too many skyscrapers and too little land area inside the city limits.
3. There is an ___overuse___ of fossil fuels when we should be looking for other natural sources of energy like wind and solar power.
4. City officials are trying to stop development in areas with ___overburdened___ roads and schools.
5. The best way to prevent the ___overflowing___ of our landfills is to have better and more efficient recycling programs.
6. Another way to help reduce the ___overcrowding___ of our schools is to build more schools and hire more teachers.

40 • Unit 7

6 Complete the conversations. Use the expressions in the box and the information in the list.

One thing to do . . .   The best way to fight . . .
Another thing to do . . .   One way to help . . .

- ☑ complain to the Parks Department about it
- ☐ create more government-funded jobs
- ☐ create more public housing projects
- ☐ educate young people about its dangers
- ☐ organize a public meeting to protest the threat to public property
- ☐ report it to the local newspaper
- ☐ donate money to charities that provide shelters and food

1. A: Did you know that a big housing developer wants to build an apartment complex in Forest Hill Park? I think it's terrible.
   B: *One thing to do is to complain to the Parks Department about it.*
   A: That's a good idea.
   B: _____

2. A: Personally, I'm worried about drug trafficking. It puts lots of children and young people at risk.
   B: _____

3. A: You know, there's a lot of corruption in our city government.
   B: _____
   A: Yeah, the bad publicity might help to clean things up a bit.

4. A: There are so many unemployed people in this city. I just don't know what can be done about it.
   B: _____

5. A: What worries me most is the number of homeless people on the streets.
   B: _____
   A: I agree.
   B: _____

a new housing development?

The world we live in • 41

7 **Complete the sentences using the present continuous passive or the present perfect passive. Then suggest a solution to each problem.**

1. Prices ___have been raised___ (raise) a lot in recent years.
   One way to deal with inflation ___is to stop pay raises___.

2. These days, a lot of endangered animals _____ (kill) by hunters and poachers. The best way to stop this practice _____.

3. During the past few years, lots of trees _____ (destroy) by acid rain. One thing to do about it is _____.

4. Underground water _____ (contaminate) by agricultural sprays. The best way to deal with the problem _____.

5. Too many young people's lives _____ (ruin) through use of illegal drugs. The best way to fight drug traffickers is _____.

8 **Write two paragraphs about a charity. In the first paragraph, describe what the charity does. In the second paragraph, explain why you think the charity is useful.**

   A good charity in my city is Shelter. This organization works to reduce the number of homeless people on our streets. Shelter believes the best way to do this is to . . .
   Shelter is my favorite charity because homelessness is, in my opinion, the greatest problem facing my city. Many people cannot find jobs, and . . .

42 • Unit 7

8 Lifelong learning

1 **Choose the correct words or phrases.**

1. I want to take a course in ___nutritional science___ because I'm interested in how diet can affect people's health. (environmental science / exercise science / nutritional science)

2. I'd prefer not to study ___archaeology___, as I'm more interested in modern life than life in the past. (archaeology / astronomy / criminology)

3. I'd really like to work in radio and television, so I'm thinking of taking a course in ___broadcasting___. (apparel manufacturing / broadcasting / film studies)

4. I'm an artistic type, so I'd rather study something like ___fashion design___ or interior design than study economics. (fashion design / hospitality / nursing)

2 **What would you prefer?**

A Write questions with *would rather* or *would prefer* using the cues.

1. take a film class/a broadcasting class
   <u>Would you rather take a film class or a broadcasting class?</u> OR
   <u>Would you prefer to take a film class or a broadcasting class?</u>

2. study part-time/full-time
   <u>Would prefer to study part-time or full-time?</u>

3. have a boring job that pays well/an exciting job that pays less
   <u>Would you rather have a boring job that pays well or an exciting job that pays less.</u>

4. take a long vacation once a year/several short vacations each year
   <u>Would you prefer to take a long vacation once a year or several short vacations each year?</u>

B Write answers to the questions you wrote in part A.

1. _____
2. _____
3. _____
4. _____

43

3 Love it or leave it

A First, complete speaker A's questions with four things you would *not* like to do. Use ideas in the box or your own ideas.

> learn to play the accordion   study criminology
> learn clothing design   take a class in nutrition
> learn how to repair watches   take a cooking class

Example:

A: Do you want to *learn to play the accordion?*
B: *I'd rather not. I'd prefer to take a class in filmmaking.* OR
   I'd prefer not to. I'd rather take a class in filmmaking.

1. A: Do you want to _____ ?
   B: _____
2. A: Would you like to _____ ?
   B: _____
3. A: Do you want to _____ ?
   B: _____
4. A: Would you like to _____ ?
   B: _____

B Now write responses for speaker B. For each question, think of something you would prefer to do. Use the short answers *I'd rather not* or *I'd prefer not to* and say what you would prefer to do.

4 Answer these questions and give reasons.

1. On your day off, would you rather stay home or go out?
   I'd rather stay home than go out because _____
2. Would you prefer to have a cat or a dog?
   _____
3. Would you prefer to live in an apartment building or in a house?
   _____
4. When you entertain friends, would you rather invite them over for dinner or take them out to a restaurant?
   _____
5. Would you prefer to see a new film at the theater or wait to see it on DVD?
   _____

5 Homeschooling

A In some countries, there are children who are educated by their parents at home instead of by teachers at school. Do you think this is a good or a bad idea? Think of two advantages and two disadvantages.

B Read the newspaper article and underline the information that answers these questions.

1. How many children in the United States learn at home?
2. Why do some parents prefer to teach their own children?
3. How do the Gutersons choose what to teach their children?
4. What are two criticisms of homeschooling?

Parents... and teachers too!

All children in the United States have to receive an education, but the law does not say they have to be educated in a school. A growing number of parents prefer not to send their children to school. Children who are educated at home are known as "homeschoolers." It is estimated that there are now between 1.5 and 1.9 million homeschoolers in the United States, about 4 percent of school-age children.

Some parents prefer to teach their children at home because they do not believe that schools teach the correct religious values. Others believe they can provide a better education for their children at home. There are now many Web sites about homeschooling, and many parents who teach their children at home use the Internet to exchange ideas and resources. Interestingly, results show that homeschooled children often do better than average on national tests in reading and math.

David Guterson and his wife teach their three children at home. Guterson says that his children learn very differently from children in school. A lesson starts with the children's interests and questions. If the Brazilian rain forests are in the news, it could start a discussion about how rain forests influence the climate, how deserts are formed, and how the polar ice caps affect ocean levels.

Homeschooling is often more interesting than going to a traditional school, but critics say that homeschoolers can become social outsiders who are uncomfortable mixing with other people in adult life. Another criticism is that many parents are not well qualified to teach. However, most parents don't have the time or the desire to teach their children at home, so most children still get their education at school.

C What could the Gutersons teach their children if the TV news showed...?

1. people without enough food to eat _____

2. a space robot landing on Mars _____

3. doctors announcing a cure for the common cold _____

D After reading the newspaper article, would you make any changes to the advantages and disadvantages you listed in part A?

6 Complete the sentences with by + gerund. Use not if needed. Use the ideas in the box or your own information.

| cook at home | eat out | go out more often | study a martial art |
| eat good food | exercise regularly | ✓stay home | use e-mail |

1. A good way to enjoy the weekend is _not by staying home but by going out with friends._
2. A good way to keep in touch with old friends is _____
3. You can make new friends _____
4. The best way to save money is _____
5. You could stay in shape _____
6. I stay healthy _____
7. One way to learn discipline _____

7 Choose the correct words or phrases.

1. Diana shows her _____ by volunteering to help people with AIDS. (competitiveness / communication skills / concern for others)

2. My parents' love of art, poetry, and music taught me _____ from a very young age. (artistic appreciation / cooperation / perseverance)

3. I learned _____ from my parents. They taught me the importance of being polite to both family and friends. (concern for others / courtesy / self-confidence)

4. Barbara always gets upset with people who disagree with her. I wish she would show more _____ . (perseverance / self-confidence / tolerance)

5. I recently joined a choir, and I love it. But you need a lot of _____ , because you have to practice the same piece of music for weeks before you're ready to perform it! (artistic appreciation / perseverance / volunteering)

46 • Unit 8

8 Personal qualities

A Read about each student in these descriptions and choose a suitable quality for each one.

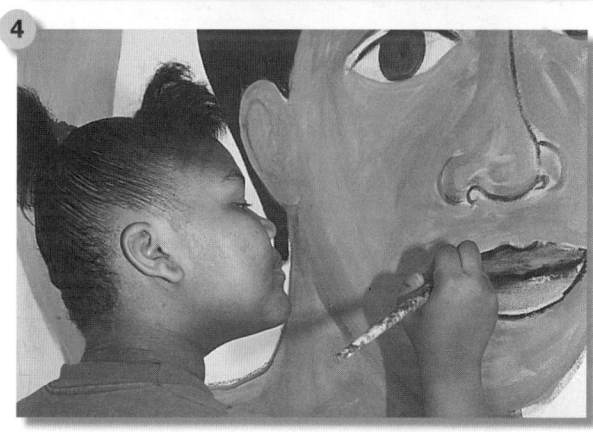

- ☐ artistic appreciation ☐ cooperation ☐ creativity ☐ self-confidence
- ☐ competitiveness ☐ courtesy ☐ perseverance ☐ tolerance

1. John is very good at most school subjects, but he has no interest in being "the best." Instead, he is very kind and helpful. The world would be a better place if everyone showed as much _____ as John.

2. Felix finds school very hard, but no one tries harder than he does. He always spends the whole weekend in the library trying to keep up with his studies. He shows great _____ .

3. Betsy always wants to do better than everyone else. In school, she always tries to get the best grades. Her favorite sport is badminton because she's the best player in the school. No one needs to teach Betsy _____ .

4. Andrea has more _____ than any of her classmates. She writes fascinating stories that show she has a wonderful imagination. She's also very artistic and does very interesting paintings.

B Write two similar descriptions of people you know. Either use the two qualities you didn't use in part A or choose other qualities.

Lifelong learning • 47

9 My way

A List two methods of learning each of these skills.

1. become a good guitarist
   by teaching myself
   by taking lessons

2. learn a new craft

3. become a good photographer

4. learn how to drive

5. become skilled at auto repair

6. learn to dance well

B Which of the two methods in part A would you prefer to use to develop each skill? Write sentences using *would rather (not)* or *would prefer (not)*. Give reasons.

1. *I'd rather learn guitar by teaching myself than by taking lessons.*
   I'd prefer not to take lessons because they're expensive.

2.

3.

4.

5.

6.

48 • Unit 8

9 At your service

1 Which service does each person need? Choose the correct word or phrase.

- ☐ dry cleaning
- ☑ essay typing
- ☐ handyman services
- ☐ house painting
- ☐ language tutoring
- ☐ pet-sitting

1. _essay typing_

   Marty: I have so many papers to write before the end of the semester! Luckily, I have all the research done and the first drafts written. I guess I can get someone to help me out just this once with my term papers.

2. _____

   Junko: I don't like the flowered wallpaper in my bedroom or the dark color of the walls in my living room. I need to have someone remove the wallpaper and make the whole place look bigger and brighter with fun, modern colors everywhere.

3. _____

   Elizabeth: Now that it's getting colder, I need to take my winter clothes out of storage. Some things I can wash in the washing machine, but I should take my wool coat to that new place around the corner.

4. _____

   David: Do you know where I can board my dog? I'm going on a two-week trip. Actually, I'd prefer someone to come to my apartment every day to play with him and feed him while I'm gone. Yeah, that's a better idea!

5. _____

   Bill: I'm so excited! I'm finally going to Quebec this summer. I studied French in high school and a little bit in college, but I'm not sure how much I remember now. Do you know where I can get someone to help me improve my French?

6. _____

   Paula: I really want to move into that studio apartment I found downtown. It's close to work and has a good view of the river. The only problem is that there are a lot of little things that I need to get repaired, such as a leaky faucet and a broken lock.

49

2 Where can I . . . ? Homework 4/13/07

A Match the verbs in column A with the nouns in column B.

A	B		
☑ check	☐ my apartment	1.	check my fitness level
☐ cut	☐ my computer	2.	_____
☐ decorate	☐ my dog	3.	_____
☐ trace	☐ my family history	4.	_____
☐ train	☑ my fitness level	5.	_____
☐ upgrade	☐ my hair	6.	_____

B First, use the items in part A to write questions for speaker A.
Use the phrases *Do you know where I can **have** someone . . . ?*
OR *Do you know where I can **get** someone to . . . ?*
Then write responses for speaker B
using your own ideas.

1. A: <u>Do you know where I can have someone check my fitness level?</u>
   B: <u>Sure. You can have it checked at the free clinic.</u>   OR
   A: <u>Do you know where I can get someone to check my fitness level?</u>
   B: <u>Sure. You can get it checked at the free clinic.</u>

passive
2. A: <u>Do you know where I can get my hair cut?</u>
   B: <u>Sure. You can have your hair cut by Hazel.</u>

active
3. A: _____
   B: _____

passive
4. A: _____
   B: _____

active
5. A: _____
   B: _____

passive
6. A: _____
   B: _____

50 • Unit 9

3
Describe where you can have these services done. Use the passive with have or get.

1. You can have your hair cut at Salon 21.   OR
   You can get your hair cut at Salon 21.

2. _____

3. _____

4. _____

4
Choose the correct three-word phrasal verb for each sentence.

1. I can't _____ that loud music anymore! I can't stand rap and I'm going to tell my neighbor right now. (cut down on / put up with / take care of)

2. My cousin didn't know what to do for her mother's 60th birthday, but she finally _____ the idea of a surprise picnic with the whole family. (came up with / got along with / looked forward to)

3. Judy has done it again! She only met Sam two months ago, and already she has _____ him. They just didn't seem to agree on anything. (broken up with / gotten along with / kept up with)

4. After Pat saw her doctor, she decided to _____ eating fast food. She wants to lose some weight and start exercising again in order to keep fit. (cut down on / look forward to / take care of)

At your service • 51

5 Feng shui goes west   Hmk 11/15/07

A Look at the picture. What do you think a person who practices feng shui does?

Feng shui

For thousands of years, the ancient art form of feng shui has played a major role in Chinese life. Feng shui means "wind and water," and it is based on an appreciation of the relationship between people and the environment. It involves changing the design of your living or working space to improve your fortune.

Soon after a Hong Kong millionaire moved his company to a new skyscraper, his business began to do badly. He called in feng shui experts, who told him that because his new building was round, it was like a cigarette – all the energy was burning off through the roof. They said that the only thing he could do to prevent this was to build a swimming pool on the roof. He followed their advice, and his business started to do well again.

In recent years, feng shui has become popular in many western countries where companies such as Nike, Citibank, and Hyatt Hotels have started to seek advice from experts. The real estate entrepreneur Donald Trump brought in a feng shui expert when he was building his famous Trump International Hotel & Tower in New York.

Does Trump believe in feng shui? He says, "It's important to adhere to the principles of a large group of people that truly believe these principles, and if they believe in them, then that's good enough for me." He admitted, "It's just another element in which you have the advantage over your competitors." Many people strongly believe in feng shui, but there are others who feel like Trump, who said, "I don't have to believe in feng shui; I do it because it makes me money."

B Read the magazine article about feng shui. Check (✓) the true statements. For statements that are false, write the true information.

1. ☐ Feng shui concerns the relationship between humans and the world around them.
   _____

2. ☐ According to feng shui, a round building is good for business.
   _____

3. ☐ Feng shui has been popular in western countries for several centuries.
   _____

4. ☐ Donald Trump used feng shui in the design of a new building in New York.
   _____

5. ☐ Trump believes in feng shui, but it makes him money, too.
   _____

C Write answers to the questions.

1. What do you think of feng shui? Is it common sense or nonsense?
   _____

2. In what circumstances would you consult a feng shui expert?
   _____

6 Make at least one suggestion for each of these problems.

1. I never have any energy, so I can never do anything except work. I sleep all weekend, so don't tell me to get more rest!

   Have you thought about *taking an aerobics class?*
   Some people say exercise gives them more energy.
   Another thing you could do is improve your diet.

2. My problem is a constant backache. I just don't know what to do to get rid of it. I had someone give me a massage, but it didn't really help.

   Maybe you could _____

3. My doctor told me to get more exercise. She strongly recommended swimming, but I find swimming so boring! In fact, aren't all sports boring?

   Why don't you _____

4. I'm very sociable, and I have great difficulty saying no. I end up doing things every night of the week – going to parties, clubs, the movies. I'm so tired all the time!

   It might be a good idea _____

5. I like to be a good neighbor, but the woman next door drives me crazy. She's always knocking on my door to chat. And whenever I go out into the yard, she goes into *her* yard – and talks for hours!

   What about _____

At your service • 53

7

Write questions for speaker A using the passive with have or get. Then write responses for speaker B using the expressions in the box.

> What about . . . ?   Why don't you . . . ?
> Have you thought about . . . ?   Maybe you could . . .

1. enlarge a photograph
   A: *Do you know where I can have a photograph enlarged?*
   B: *What about taking it to a camera shop?*

2. repair a bicycle
   A: _____
   B: _____

3. fix an MP3 player
   A: _____
   B: _____

4. shorten pants
   A: _____
   B: _____

5. replace a laptop battery
   A: _____
   B: _____

6. organize a wedding reception
   A: _____
   B: _____

10 The past and the future

1 *Choose the correct words to complete the sentences.*

1. Captain James Cook led three _____expeditions_____ to the Pacific and Antarctica from 1768 to 1779. (assassinations / expeditions / revolutions)
2. Three scientific advances took place during the mid-1890s: the _____ of X-rays, radioactivity, and the electron. (discoveries / explorations / inventions)
3. The _____ of the audio CD in 1983 led to the development of CD-ROMs and DVDs. (exploration / invention / population)
4. Landing a spacecraft on Mars in 1997 was a great _____ in space technology. (achievement / disaster / terrorist act)
5. In 2003, a powerful earthquake struck Bam, Iran. It was _____ for people living in the area. (a disaster / an assassination / a population)
6. No one knows why many ships and planes have disappeared in the Bermuda Triangle. It's still _____ . (a discovery / an epidemic / a mystery)

2 *Complete the sentences. Use words from the list.*

| ago | during | for | from | in | since | to |

1. Jazz first **became** popular __in__ the 1920s.
2. The cell phone was invented over 30 years __ago__ .
3. Brasília has been the capital city of Brazil __since__ 1960.
4. The first laptop was produced __in__ 1981.
5. Mexico has been independent __for__ more than 200 years.
6. World War II lasted __from__ 1939 __to__ 1945.
7. Vietnam was separated into two parts __for__ about 30 years.
8. East and West Germany have been united __since__ the Berlin Wall came down.

jazz

the Berlin Wall

55

Hmwk

3 Nouns and verbs

A Complete this chart. Then check your answers in a dictionary.

Noun	Verb	Noun	Verb
assassination	*assassinate*	explosion	_____
demonstrate	_____	invention	_____
discovery	_____	revolution	_____
discrimination	_____	segregation	_____
existence	_____	transformation	_____
exploration	_____	vaccine	_____

B Choose verbs from the chart in part A to complete these sentences. Use the correct verb tense.

1. In 1885, Louis Pasteur _____*discovered*_____ a cure for rabies when he treated a young boy who was bitten by a dog.

2. In World War I, many soldiers were _____ against the disease typhoid.

3. Aung San, the man who led Myanmar to independence, was _____ in 1947. No one is certain who killed him.

4. The European Union has _____ since 1957. There are now 25 member states.

5. Until the 1960s, there were many laws that _____ against African Americans in certain regions of the United States.

6. In 2003, many Venezuelans _____ against the government of President Chavez in the streets of Caracas.

7. In recent years, teams of experts in countries such as Cambodia and Angola have safely been _____ mines in order to rid those countries of these dangerous weapons.

8. One of the few parts of the world that has not been _____ much is Antarctica. The extreme climate makes it dangerous to travel far from research centers.

Louis Pasteur (1822–1895)

a research station in Antarctica

56 • Unit 10

4 Vaccines past, present, and future

A Have you ever had a vaccination? Do you know what diseases you have been vaccinated against?

VACCINATIONS

For well over a thousand years, smallpox was a disease that everyone feared. The disease killed much of the native population in South America when the Spanish arrived there in the early sixteenth century. By the end of the eighteenth century, smallpox was responsible for the deaths of about one in ten people around the world. Those who survived the disease were left with ugly scars on their skin.

It had long been well known among farmers that people who worked with cows rarely caught smallpox; instead, they often caught a similar but much milder disease called cowpox. A British doctor named Edward Jenner was fascinated by this, and so he studied cowpox. He became convinced that, by injecting people with cowpox, he could protect them against the much worse disease smallpox. In 1796, he vaccinated a boy with cowpox and, two months later, with smallpox. The boy did not get smallpox. In the next two years, Jenner vaccinated several children in the same way, and none of them got the disease.

News of Jenner's success soon spread. In 1800, the Royal Vaccine Institution was founded in Berlin, Germany. In the following year, Napoleon opened a similar institute in Paris, France. Vaccination soon became a common method to protect people against other viral diseases, such as rabies, and vaccines were sent across the world to the United States and India.

It took nearly two centuries to achieve Jenner's dream of ridding the world of smallpox. In 1967, the World Health Organization (WHO) started an ambitious vaccination program, and the last known case of smallpox was recorded in Somalia in 1977. The story of vaccinations does not end there, however. There are many other diseases that kill more and more people every year. In addition, many new diseases are being discovered. The challenge for medical researchers will, therefore, probably continue for several more centuries.

B Read the article about vaccinations. Complete the chart with the history of events in the story of vaccinations.

Date	Event
1. Early 16th century	Smallpox killed much of the native population in South America.
2. End of the 18th century	
3. 1796	
4. 1800	
5. 1967	
6. 1977	

C Imagine that vaccines are invented against three major diseases in the coming decade. Which diseases do you predict they will protect people from?

5 Life in 2050

A Complete these predictions about life in 2050. Use the future continuous of the verb given. Then add two more predictions of your own.

life on the moon?

By 2050, . . .

1. some people _will be living_ in cities on the moon. (live)

2. many people _____ temperature-controlled body suits. (wear)

3. most people _____ cars that run on fuel from garbage. (drive)

4. people _____ in a new Olympic event – mind reading. (compete)

5. _____

6. _____

B Complete these predictions about what will have happened by 2050. Use the future perfect. Then add two more predictions of your own.

By 2050, . . .

1. computers _will have replaced_ people as translators. (replace)

2. ties for men _____ out of fashion. (go)

3. scientists _____ a cheap way of getting drinking water from seawater. (discover)

4. medical researchers _____ a cure for cancer. (find)

5. _____

6. _____

a cure for cancer?

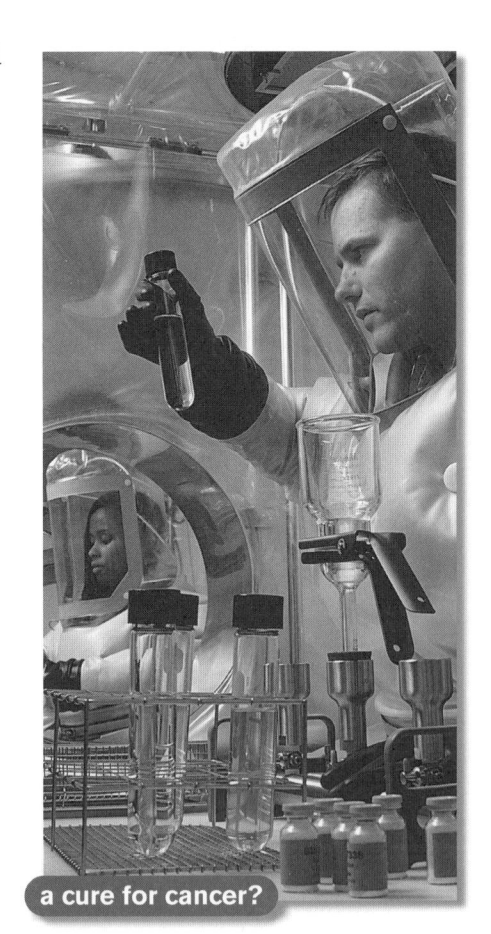

58 • Unit 10

6 Write two responses to each question.

1. What will or won't you be doing in ten years? (Use the future continuous.)
   I won't be living with my parents.

2. How will cities of the future be different? (Use *will*.)
   Cities won't allow cars downtown.

3. How will life in small villages in your country have changed in the next 20 years? (Use the future.)
   People will be connected to big cities by the Internet.

4. How do you think the world's weather will change during this century? (Use *will*.)
   The weather will be warmer and the summers longer.

5. What advances will scientists have made by 2050? (Use the future perfect.)
   Scientists will have found a way to grow enough food for everyone.

7 *Think of four ways that computers will affect how we live and work in the next 20 years.*

Example: <u>Children will be doing all their schoolwork on computers.</u>

1. _____
2. _____
3. _____
4. _____

8 *Write two paragraphs about one of these topics or a topic of your choice. In the first paragraph, describe the past. In the second paragraph, describe how you think the future will be.*

Topics	
a music group	computers
changes within a country	health
changes within a region	space exploration

> The European Union, or E.U., was founded in 1957. At first, there were only six member states, including France, Italy, and West Germany. Nine other countries joined during the next 40 years. Many European nations came together because they wanted to avoid another world war.
>
> The E.U. has continued to develop during the twenty-first century. In 2002, nearly all the member states adopted the same currency — the euro. In 2004, ten more countries joined the E.U. In the future, the nations of the E.U. will continue to develop economic, political, and social cooperation. In the near future, several more countries, such as Bulgaria, Romania, and Turkey, will probably join the E.U.

11 Life's little lessons

1 Milestones

A Read these statements. Check (✓) the ones that are true for you. For statements that are false, write the true information.

Example: As soon as I got my first cell phone, I called all my friends.
The moment I got a cell phone, I called my parents. OR
I've never had a cell phone.

1. ☐ By the time I was three years old, I had already learned two languages.
___

2. ☐ Before I started school, I was carefree – I used to watch TV all day.
___

3. ☐ After I started taking the bus by myself, I became more independent.
___

4. ☐ As soon as I got my driver's license, my parents let me drive everywhere.
___

5. ☐ The moment I discovered the Internet, I signed up for an e-mail account.
___

6. ☐ Once I started learning English, I quit studying other languages.
___

7. ☐ Until I graduated from high school, I was very unsophisticated.
___

8. ☐ Before I became more independent, I thought I knew more than my parents.
___

B Write three true statements about yourself, your family, or your friends.

1. ___
2. ___
3. ___

61

2 Complete these descriptions. Use words from the list.

- ☐ ambitious
- ☐ carefree
- ☐ rebellious
- ☐ argumentative
- ☐ generous
- ☑ sophisticated

1. Kate is so _____sophisticated_____. She always dresses well, she knows lots of intelligent people, and she never says anything silly.

2. I just spent a horrible evening with Gloria. She questioned and criticized everything I said. I wish she weren't so _____.

3. My sister is very _____. She never forgets her friends' birthdays and always gives them nice gifts.

4. Once I turned 16, I became less _____, and my parents started to let me do what I wanted.

5. Paul is really _____. He wants to own his own business by the time he's 25.

6. I wish I could be like Debbie. She's so _____ and never seems to worry about anything.

3 Do you have a friend who is special to you? Write about him or her. In the first paragraph, describe the person. In the second paragraph, describe a particular time when the person helped you.

> One of my best friends is Christine. She's very mature and conscientious, and she always gives me good advice. Until I met her, I had been making some bad decisions. . . .
>
> Christine is also very generous. She always helps her friends when they need it. For example, the moment she found out I was sick last winter, she came over and cooked dinner for me.

62 • Unit 11

4 Turning points

A Have you had any major turning points in your life? If so, what were they? If not, are there any major changes you would like to make?

Lance Armstrong

Lance Armstrong was born in Plano, Texas, in 1971. As a child, he enjoyed running, swimming, and bicycling – and when he was only 13, he competed in his first **triathlon**. He became a professional athlete at age 16. While he was still in high school, the American national cycling team asked Armstrong to work out with them.

In 1991, Armstrong won several major races. However, he didn't always win. At the 1992 Barcelona Olympics, he finished fourteenth – a poor showing. The next year, he made a fantastic **comeback**: He won the U.S. cycling "Triple Crown," and then became the youngest cyclist ever to win the World Race Championships in Norway.

Armstrong's career was really taking off. Then in 1996, he started to feel tired and ill. He finished in only twelfth place in the Atlanta Olympics – a disappointment. Later that year, Armstrong got the shock of his life: He was diagnosed with cancer, and his doctors said he had only a 40 percent chance of surviving. Many people were convinced that his career was over.

Armstrong would not quit. He had surgery and chemotherapy, and by February 1997, he was cancer-free. With his cancer in **remission**, he was determined to train hard and compete again with the world's top cyclists.

In 1998, Armstrong returned to professional racing. He wanted to be the best, and that meant he had to win the most **prestigious** race in the world: the Tour de France. No one thought he could recover from cancer and win such a **strenuous** race. Armstrong proved them wrong: Not only did he win it in 1999, but he also won it every year for another five years!

Many consider Armstrong to be one of the world's greatest athletes, and a real **inspiration**. Armstrong once wrote: "I don't always win. Sometimes just finishing is the best I can do. But with each race, I feel that I further define my capacity for living. That's why I ride, and why I try to ride hard, even when I don't have to."

B Read the sports magazine article about Lance Armstrong. Look at the words in **bold** in the article. Can you write definitions or synonyms for each word?

1. triathlon _____
2. comeback _____
3. remission _____
4. prestigious _____
5. strenuous _____
6. inspiration _____

C What are two turning points for each of the time periods in Armstrong's life?

1991–1995 _Armstrong won the National Amateur Cycling Championship in 1991._

1996–1997 _____

1998–2004 _____

D What do you think about Lance Armstrong's decision to continue as a professional athlete after he was diagnosed with cancer? Do you think he is an inspiration?

Life's little lessons • 63

5 Regrets

A Write sentences about each person's regret. Use *should (not) have*.

1. Eric was very argumentative with his boss, so she fired him.
   Eric shouldn't have been argumentative with his boss.

2. Marsha changed jobs. Now she works in a bank. Working in a large company is more interesting.

3. Ivan worked seven days a week for several years. Then he got very sick.

4. Carla refused every job offer she received. She's been unemployed for a year, and she no longer gets any job offers.

5. Andrew studied music in school, but he's much better at computer science.

6. Jim was completely rebellious when he was a student, so he got very bad grades.

7. Frances spent too much money on clothes. Now she can't afford to take a vacation.

8. Judy was very naive when she was younger. She often lent money to people, but they never repaid her.

B Write about your own regrets. Write four sentences with *should (not) have*.

1.
2.
3.
4.

6 If . . .

A Rewrite the sentences as hypothetical situations. Use the words given.

1. I should have studied English sooner. (get a better job)
   If I'd studied English sooner, I would have gotten a better job.

2. We should have made a reservation. (eat already)
   _____

3. You should have let me drive. (arrive by now)
   _____

4. I should have studied harder. (pass my exams)
   _____

5. I should have been more sensible. (save more money)
   _____

B Write sentences describing hypothetical situations. Use the words given and your own ideas.

1. argumentative _If I'd been less argumentative as a child,_
   I would have had a better relationship with my parents.

2. ambitious _____

3. mature or immature _____

4. naive _____

5. rebellious _____

6. conscientious _____

Life's little lessons • 65

7 Complete the conversation. Circle the correct time expressions and use the correct tense of the verbs given.

Andy: I've made such a mess of my life!

John: What do you mean?

Andy: If I ____hadn't accepted____ (not accept) a job (**as soon as**/ before / until) I graduated, I _____ (travel) around Europe all summer – just like you did. You were so carefree.

John: You know, I should _____ (not go) to Europe. I should _____ (take) the great job I was offered. (After / Before / Until) I returned from Europe, it was too late.

Andy: But my job is so depressing! (Before / The moment / Until) I started it, I hated it – on the very first day! That was five years ago, and nothing's changed. I should _____ (look) for another job right away.

John: Well, start looking now. There were some good jobs advertised on the Internet last month. If I _____ (not check) the Internet, I _____ (not see) this great job listing.

Andy: Really? What's the job?

John: It's working as a landscape gardener. (Before / The moment / Until) I saw it, I knew it was right for me.

Andy: But for me right now, the problem is I get a very good salary, and I just bought a house. If I _____ (not buy) the house, I _____ (be able to) take a lower paying job.

John: Well, I guess you can't have everything. If I _____ (have) a better salary, I _____ (buy) a house, too.

66 • Unit 11

12 The right stuff

1 **Complete these sentences with In order for or In order to.**

1. _In order for_ a restaurant to be popular, it has to have attractive decor.
2. _____ a movie to be entertaining, it has to have good actors and an interesting story.
3. _____ succeed in business, you often have to work long hours.
4. _____ attract new members, a sports club needs to offer inexpensive memberships.
5. _____ speak a foreign language well, it's a good idea to use the language as often as possible.
6. _____ a travel agency to succeed, it has to be able to find the cheapest airline tickets.

a popular restaurant

2 **Write sentences. Use the information in the box.**

- ☐ have talented salespeople
- ☑ keep up with your studies
- ☐ be clever and entertaining
- ☐ work extremely long hours
- ☐ provide excellent customer service
- ☐ have informative and well-written articles

1. be a successful student
   In order to be a successful student, you have to keep up with your studies.
2. a clothes store to be profitable
   For a clothes store to be profitable, _____
3. manage your own business
   _____
4. an advertisement to be persuasive
   _____
5. run a successful automobile company
   _____
6. a magazine to be successful
   _____

67

3 Choose the correct word or phrase.

1. I didn't enjoy this book on how to succeed in business. It wasn't very ___well written___ . (affordable / well typed / well written)

2. I learned a lot about how to run a successful bookstore from reading that magazine. I found it very _____ . (attractive / informative / knowledgeable)

3. Linda has so many interesting ideas, and she's always thinking of new projects. She's very _____ . (clever / patient / tough)

4. Rosie is a salesperson, and she's good at her job. She's so _____ that she sells three times as much as her co-workers. (friendly / gorgeous / persuasive)

5. Daniel is one of the top models in Milan. He goes to the gym every day so he looks really _____ . (clever / fashionable / muscular)

6. For a restaurant to succeed, it has to _____ a high level of quality in both food and service. (keep up with / maintain / put up with)

7. If a department store improves its _____ and looks really fashionable, it can attract a lot of new customers. (boutique / decor / safety record)

4 Read this information about journalists. Then write a paragraph about one of the people from the list or another person of your choice.

> To be a successful journalist, you need to be both talented and dynamic. You have to write well and write quickly. In order to report the news, a journalist needs to have a good knowledge of world and current events. In addition, you must be able to report a story accurately.

an artist   a boss   a homemaker   a parent   a teacher

68 • Unit 12

5 I like it because . . .

A For each pair of pictures, write one sentence about what you like and one sentence about what you dislike. Give reasons using the words given.

1.

I like this park because it's clean and there are a lot of trees. (because)

I don't like this park since _____ (since)

2.

_____ (since)

_____ (the reason)

3.

_____ (because of)

_____ (due to)

B Think of an example in your city of each of these places: a restaurant, a hotel, a shopping center. Write a sentence about why you like or dislike each one.

Example: *The reason I don't like Cho Dang Gol Restaurant in my hometown is its noisy location right by the freeway.*

1. _____
2. _____
3. _____

The right stuff • **69**

6 Success story

A Think of a successful company. Why is it successful?

BUSINESS as unusual

The Body Shop International operates in 12 time zones, 25 languages, and 50 countries around the world. The company now has more than 1,900 stores selling five products every two seconds. It now has a range of more than 600 products and 400 **accessories**. This is a major achievement, since The Body Shop started in 1976 with just one **outlet** in Britain. The original store had only about 25 homemade products for sale. Most of the ingredients, such as aloe vera and jojoba oil, were not widely known at the time.

The founder of The Body Shop is the entrepreneur Anita Roddick. Roddick had a vision not just of making money, but of developing new beauty products without testing them on animals. It is estimated that more than 35,000 animals are used every year in the European Union in tests on cosmetic products. Common tests include dripping liquids into rabbits' eyes and **force-feeding** them with test substances. Roddick says her company never has, and never will, use animals for research purposes because she believes these practices are cruel.

Another central feature of Roddick's philosophy is the creation of trading relationships with communities in developing countries. Her objective is to provide income for these communities by paying reasonable prices for **raw materials** and accessories. Raw materials include cocoa butter, which is used in hand and body lotions, and accessories include foot massagers from southern India and back-scrubbing products from Honduras.

The Body Shop's belief – that business is primarily about human relationships and respect for the natural world – seems to be popular with customers. Not only has the company grown quickly, but it is also widely seen as **reputable**. Recently, the company was voted the second best retail company worldwide. Roddick's practices may not be **conventional wisdom** for success in business, but they have certainly worked for The Body Shop.

B Read the article in a newsletter for new business owners. Look at the words in **bold** in the article. Can you write definitions or synonyms for each word?

1. accessories _____
2. outlet _____
3. force-feeding _____
4. raw materials _____
5. reputable _____
6. conventional wisdom _____

C In what ways is The Body Shop an unusual company? Can you think of another company that has a similar philosophy to that of Anita Roddick? What do you think of this philosophy?

70 • *Unit 12*

7
Look at these advertisements and write two sentences about each one. Describe the features and give reasons why you like or dislike the advertisements.

1

OUR BASIC CONCEPT

FORD RANGER starting at $11,080

BUILT FORD TOUGH

Advertisement used with permission from Ford.

3

Presenting the 10 calorie, fat free cookie.

(Actual size)

Presenting 10 calorie, fat free Jell-O.

(Actual size)

Even fat free snacks can be loaded with calories. So why settle for just a bite? Sugar Free Strawberry Kiwi Jell-O Gelatin.

Sugar Free JELL-O

Advertisement used with permission from Kraft Foods.

2

School's Open

Drive Carefully!

SPONSORED BY YOUR AAA CLUB

Advertisement used with permission from the American Automobile Association.

Example: *A nice thing about the first ad is that it attracts your attention. I like it because of the clever concept.*

1. _____

2. _____

3. _____

The right stuff • **71**

8 Complete this crossword puzzle.

Across

3 For a salesperson to be persuasive, he or she has to be _____ with words.

5 The big supermarket _____ are causing many small local stores to close.

7 In order for sports clubs to remain popular, they must have the most modern _____ , such as treadmills and stair climbers.

9 To be _____ , successful male models work out daily with trainers.

10 Maybe I'm old-fashioned, but I don't like the latest _____ in clothes.

12 I don't have a favorite _____ of clothing. Designer clothes are too expensive, so I just buy cheap clothes that look good on me.

13 I like the family-owned shop on my street because it always has interesting _____ products that I've never seen before.

14 I don't know why Gloria doesn't try modeling. She is absolutely _____ .

Down

1 For a coffee shop to make enough money to be _____ in my neighborhood, it has to attract young people and stay open late.

2 The Leo Jazz Club has a great new band. I've heard they're very _____ musicians.

4 Due to its boring content, *Weekend Talk* ran for only three months. For a TV show to be successful on Saturday evenings, it really has to be _____ .

6 I wouldn't be a good _____ because I'm not very persuasive.

8 While I was waiting in the doctor's office, I read a fantastic new _____ . I liked it so much that I decided to buy it every month from now on.

11 For a clothing boutique to be profitable, the salespeople have to be charming and _____ to make sure that enough customers buy clothes.

13 That's a possibility.

1 What do you think happened? Write an explanation for each event using past modals.

1. *Someone might have broken into the house.*
2. _____
3. _____
4. _____
5. _____
6. _____
7. _____

73

2
Write two paragraphs about something strange that has happened to you. In the first paragraph, describe the situation. In the second paragraph, give two or three explanations for what happened.

> I invited six friends to a barbecue on the beach. I suggested we meet at eight o'clock. They all said they would come and bring some food.
> On the day of the barbecue, only two of my friends showed up. I guess my other friends could have overslept, or they might have decided to do something else. Another possibility is that they may have thought I meant 8 P.M. instead of 8 A.M. I'm not sure what happened!

3
Answer these questions. Write two explanations using past modals.

Why do you think the ancient Britons built Stonehenge?

1. They might have _built it to use as a church._

2. _____

3. They could have _____

4. _____

How do you think early explorers communicated with people in the places they visited?

What do you think happened immediately after the *Titanic* hit the iceberg?

5. People may have _____

6. _____

74 • Unit 13

4 Strange creatures

A Some cultures have ancient stories about strange creatures similar to humans. For example, in Scandinavia, some people believe that small creatures called elves live in the forests.

Are there any legends like this in your country? What are they?

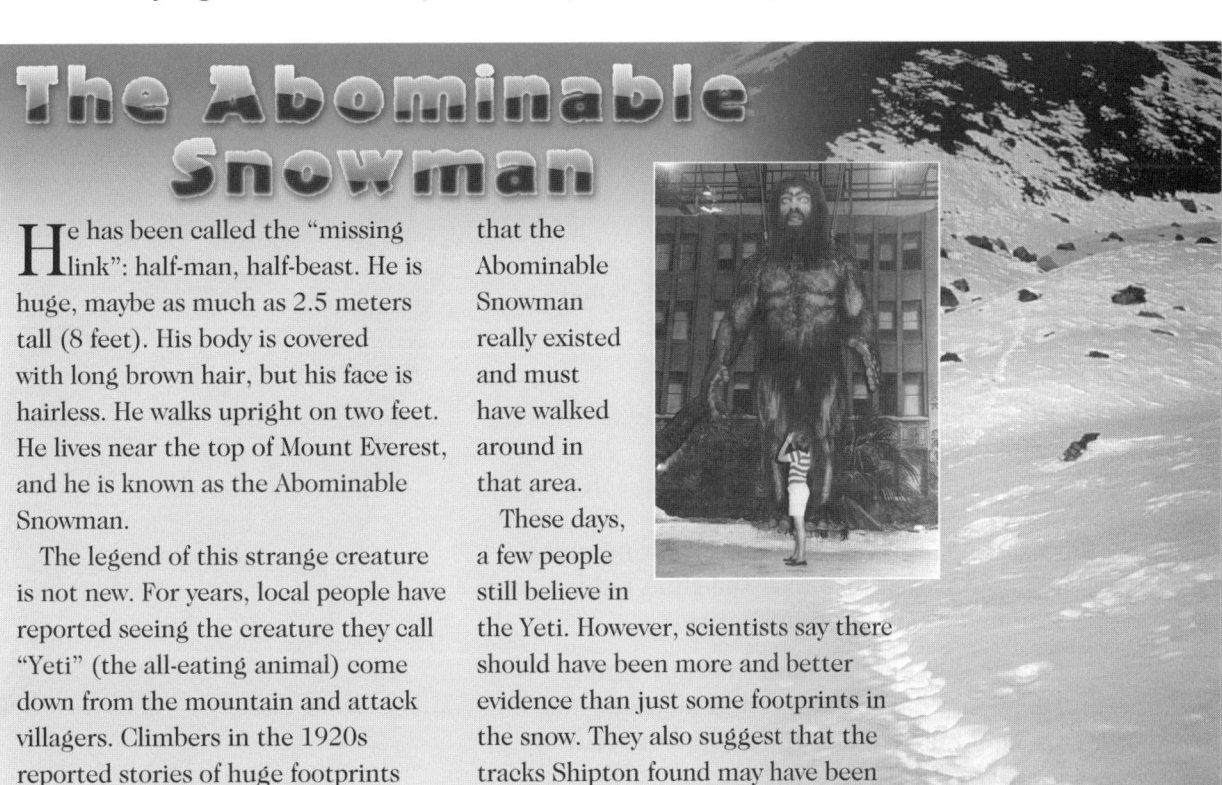

The Abominable Snowman

He has been called the "missing link": half-man, half-beast. He is huge, maybe as much as 2.5 meters tall (8 feet). His body is covered with long brown hair, but his face is hairless. He walks upright on two feet. He lives near the top of Mount Everest, and he is known as the Abominable Snowman.

The legend of this strange creature is not new. For years, local people have reported seeing the creature they call "Yeti" (the all-eating animal) come down from the mountain and attack villagers. Climbers in the 1920s reported stories of huge footprints they saw high in the Himalayas – footprints unlike any other animal. In 1951, the explorer Eric Shipton took photographs of enormous tracks in the snow of Mount Everest. He assumed that the Abominable Snowman really existed and must have walked around in that area.

These days, a few people still believe in the Yeti. However, scientists say there should have been more and better evidence than just some footprints in the snow. They also suggest that the tracks Shipton found may have been only bear tracks. However, if anyone ever succeeds in catching an Abominable Snowman, they may face a real problem: Would they put it in a zoo or give it a room in a hotel?

B Read the encyclopedia article about a world-famous legend. Then write answers to the questions.

1. How could someone describe the Abominable Snowman?

2. What's another name for the Abominable Snowman?

3. In 1951, what "evidence" did Shipton find, and how did he record it?

4. Why don't many scientists believe Shipton found tracks of the Abominable Snowman?

C Do you think the Abominable Snowman exists? If yes, do you think it is man or beast?

That's a possibility. • 75

5 Should have, could have, would have

A What should or shouldn't these people have done?
Read each situation and check (✓) the best suggestion.

1. Joe's old car broke down on the highway late one night. He left the car on the side of the road and walked home.

   ☐ He should have stopped a stranger's car to ask for a ride.
   ☐ He could have slept in his car till morning.
   ☐ He should have walked to the nearest pay phone and called a tow truck.

2. Linda was in a park. She saw some people leave all their trash after they had finished their picnic. She did nothing.

   ☐ She did the right thing.
   ☐ She should have asked them to throw away their trash.
   ☐ She could have thrown away the trash herself.

3. John saw a three-year-old child walking alone in a shopping mall. He took the child to his home and immediately called the police.

   ☐ He shouldn't have taken the child home.
   ☐ He should have left the child alone.
   ☐ He could have taken the child to a security guard in the mall.

4. Mrs. Judd wouldn't let her children watch TV for a month because they broke a window playing baseball.

   ☐ She could have made them pay for the window.
   ☐ She shouldn't have done anything. It was an accident.
   ☐ She shouldn't have let them play baseball for a month.

5. Martha's boss borrowed $20 from her a month ago but he forgot to pay her back. Martha never said anything about it.

   ☐ She should have demanded her money back.
   ☐ She shouldn't have loaned it to him.
   ☐ She could have written him a nice note asking for the money.

B What would you have done in the situations in part A?
Write suggestions or comments using past modals.

1. *I would have called a friend to give me a ride home.*
2. _____
3. _____
4. _____
5. _____

76 • Unit 13

6 Nouns and verbs

A Complete the chart.

Noun	Verb	Noun	Verb
advice	*advise*	excuse	_____
_____	assume	_____	predict
criticism	_____	suggestion	_____
_____	demand	_____	warn

B Complete the sentences using words from the chart in part A. For the verbs, use *shouldn't have* + past participle. For the nouns, use the appropriate singular or plural form.

1. I ___*shouldn't have excused*___ you last time! Don't you ever ride my motorcycle without my permission again.

2. Bart bought an expensive ring and gave it to Millie for her birthday. A year later, he asked her to marry him. When she said no, he made an outrageous _____. He said he wanted his ring back!

3. Justin _____ having a beach party. It was so cold that we all got sick.

4. Phil _____ I would still be awake at midnight. I was asleep when he called.

5. Jill said she was late because she got caught in traffic. Hmm! I've heard that _____ before.

6. The weather report said it would rain today. That _____ was completely wrong. It's been sunny all day.

7. My professor _____ me to take a course in English literature. I have absolutely no interest in it.

8. Josh _____ me for wearing jeans and a T-shirt to a friend's party.

That's a possibility. • 77

7 Complete these conversations. Use past modals in the box and the verbs given. (More than one modal is possible.)

could have
may have
might have
must have
should have

1. A: Where's Alex? He's late.
   B: He _may have gotten_ (get) stuck in rush-hour traffic.
   A: He's always late! You know, he _should have bought_ (buy) a new cell phone last month when they had that special. Then he could let us know what the problem is.

2. A: Nina never responded to my invitation.
   B: She _____ (not receive) it.
   You _____ (call) her.

3. A: Jeff hasn't answered his phone for a week.
   B: He _____ (go) on vacation.
   He _____ (tell) you, though – sometimes he's very inconsiderate.

4. A: I can never get in touch with Susan. She never returns phone calls or answers e-mails!
   B: Yeah, I have the same problem with her. Her voice mail _____ (run out) of space. She _____ (get) a new phone service by now.

5. A: Martin is strange. Sometimes he works really hard, but sometimes he seems pretty lazy. Last week, he hardly did any work.
   B: Well, you know, he _____ (not feel) well.
   Still, he _____ (tell) you that he was sick.

6. A: I ordered a book over the Internet a month ago, but it still hasn't arrived.
   B: They _____ (have) a problem with the warehouse, but they _____ (let) you know.

14 Behind the scenes

1 **Complete the conversation. Use the passive form of the verbs given.**

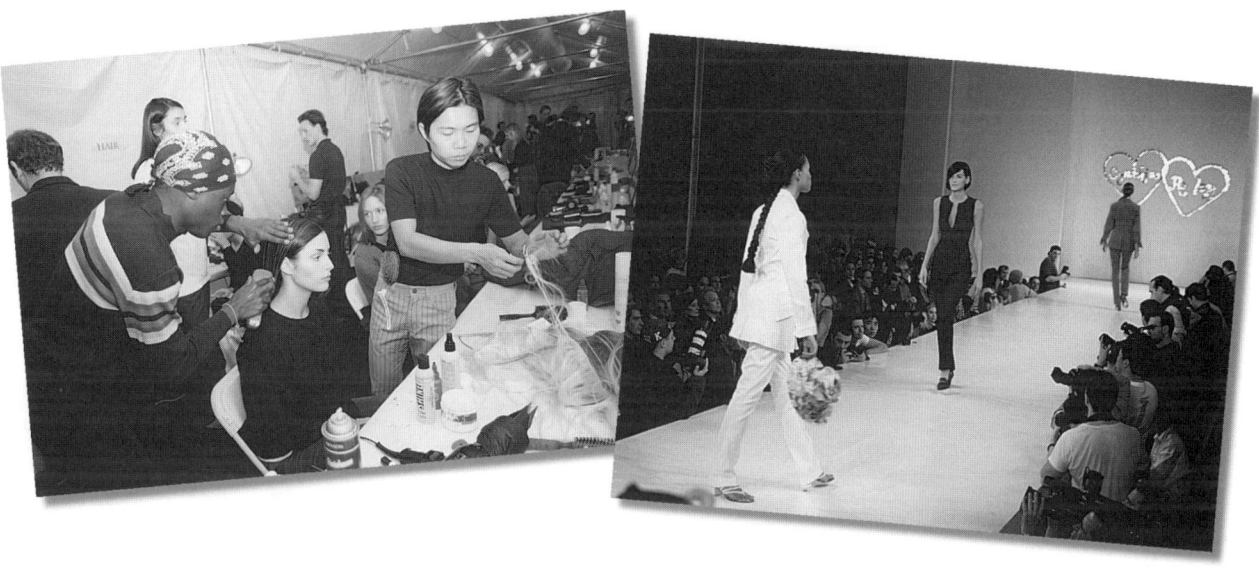

Vera: Putting on a fashion show must be really challenging!

Isaac: Yeah, but it's also fun. All the clothes have to _be numbered_ (number) so that the models wear them in the right sequence. And they also have to _____ (mark) with the name of the right model.

Vera: What happens if something _____ (wear) by the wrong model?

Isaac: Well, if it doesn't fit, it looks terrible! First impressions are very important. A lot of clothes _____ (sell) because they look good at the show.

Vera: Do you have to rehearse for a fashion show?

Isaac: Of course! There's more involved than just models and clothes. Special lighting _____ (use), and music _____ (play) during the show.

Vera: It sounds complicated.

Isaac: Oh, it is. And at some fashion shows, a commentary may _____ (give).

Vera: A commentary? What do you mean?

Isaac: Well, someone talks about the clothes as they _____ (show) on the runway by the models.

Vera: It sounds like timing is really important.

Isaac: Exactly. Everything has to _____ (time) perfectly! Otherwise, the show may _____ (ruin).

79

2 Choose the correct words or phrases.

1. Often, special music has to be _____ for a film.
   (composed / designed / hired)

2. A play may be _____ for several weeks before it is shown to the public.
   (shot / taken / rehearsed)

3. Designing _____ for actors to wear requires a lot of creativity.
   (scripts / sets / costumes)

4. Newspapers are _____ to stores after they are printed.
   (expanded / distributed / reported)

5. _____ are added after the film has been put together.
   (Preparations / Sound effects / Takes)

3 Complete this passage. Use the passive form of the verbs given.

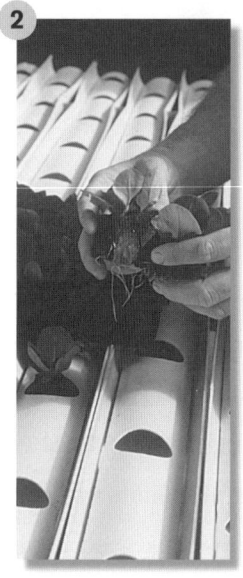

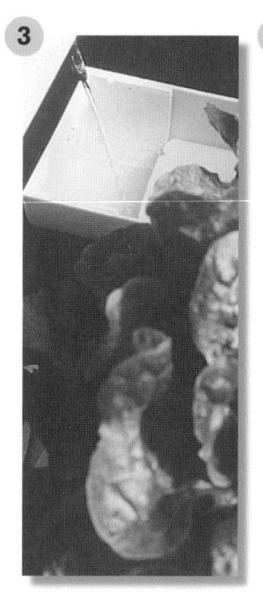

1. Nowadays, all sorts of things ___are produced___ (produce) in factories, including lettuce! At one food factory, fresh green lettuce _____ (grow) without sunlight or soil. Here is how it _____ (do).

2. Lettuce seedlings _____ (place) at one end of a long production line. Conveyor belts _____ (use) to move the seedlings slowly along. The tiny plants _____ (expose) to light from fluorescent lamps.

3. They have to _____ (feed) through the roots with plant food and water that _____ (control) by a computer.

4. Thirty days later, the plants _____ (collect) at the other end of the conveyor belts.

5. They may _____ (deliver) to the vegetable market the same day.

4 A puppet show

A Have you ever seen a puppet show? What was it like? Did you enjoy it?

International puppets

The first puppets are thought to have been used in India over 4,000 years ago. Since then, different kinds of puppets have become popular around the world.

Hand puppets are usually about 50 cm (20 inches) tall. Their main feature is a large head that has a costume with arms attached to it. These puppets are worn like a glove. The puppeteer, who stands below the stage, operates the puppet with his or her fingers. Hand puppets are widely used in European countries, such as Italy, France, and Britain.

Rod puppets have long been used in Japan and Italy and are now very popular in Eastern Europe. They are similar in shape to hand puppets but are much bigger – sometimes over 1 meter (40 inches) tall. The puppeteer, who works from below the stage, operates the puppet with rods that are attached to it: a thick rod fixed to the puppet's back, and thinner rods fixed to its neck, head, and arms. The puppeteer, holding the thick rod in one hand and the thinner rods in the other hand, can move the parts separately.

Shadow puppets are similar to rod puppets but are unique in that they are flat and much smaller – about 50 cm (20 inches). In addition, they are seen by audiences in a completely different way – these puppets appear as shadows on a screen that is lit from behind. They are controlled either from below or beside the stage. Shadow puppets, which originally came from China and Indonesia, later became popular in Turkey and Greece.

Marionettes are puppets that are constructed from several small parts. Their height varies, and they are moved by strings that are controlled from above. Many marionettes are hung on nine strings, but there are some in Myanmar that have up to 60 strings. They can be made to perform interesting tricks, such as blowing smoke from a pipe.

shadow puppet

B Read the article about different types of puppets. Complete the chart.

	Hand puppets	Rod puppets	Shadow puppets	Marionettes
Size				
How constructed?				
How moved?				
Position of puppeteer				
Where commonly used				

C How many of these types of puppets have you seen? Why do you think children love puppets?

5 Join these sentences with who or that. Add a comma wherever one is needed.

Examples:

Foreign correspondents are journalists.

They report on a particular part of the world.

Foreign correspondents are journalists that report on a particular part of the world.

A junior newspaper reporter has to do a lot of research on news stories.

He or she is often new to journalism.

A junior newspaper reporter, who is often new to journalism, has to do a lot of research on news stories.

1. A photo editor selects only the best photos for the newspaper.
   He or she tells the photographers what news stories to cover.

2. A Web-page designer is a skilled artist.
   He or she creates computer files with text, sound, and graphics for the Internet.

3. A support technician is a skilled person.
   He or she responds to calls from people with computer problems.

4. Fashion models have to make designer clothes look good.
   They are almost always young and slender.

5. TV sitcoms include actors and actresses.
   They are recognized by television viewers around the world.

6 Match the definitions with the jobs.

1. a cinematographer _g_
2. a film editor ____
3. a gossip columnist ____
4. a graphic designer ____
5. a location scout ____
6. a stagehand ____
7. a stunt person ____
8. a talk-show host ____

a. a journalist who specializes in reporting on the personal lives of famous people
b. someone who looks for places to shoot scenes in a film
c. someone that helps a movie director put together the best "takes"
d. a person who does dangerous scenes in a movie in place of the main actor
e. a TV personality who invites guests to come on his or her program
f. a person who moves sets and furniture for theater and film productions
g. a person who operates the main camera during shooting
h. someone that creates the design for a printed work

7 Choose one of the jobs in Exercise 6 or another job you're interested in. In the first paragraph, describe the job and why you would like to have it. In the second paragraph, describe what the job involves behind the scenes. Use relative clauses in some of your descriptions.

> If I worked in journalism, I'd like to be a foreign correspondent like Christiane Amanpour. These days, foreign correspondents, who are on call 24 hours a day, often work for both a newspaper and a broadcasting company. They meet and interview famous people all over the world. I would enjoy . . .
>
> Behind the scenes, foreign correspondents are members of news teams, which include technicians and camera operators. Together, they ensure that their organization receives news of important world events as soon as they happen, and, if possible, before any competitors! Foreign correspondents also have to . . .

8 **Describe six steps in the process of renovating a restaurant. Use the words in the pictures, and the passive form of the verbs given below.**

1. designer
2. builders
3. painters
4. electrician
5. delivery people
6. owner

1. First, *an interior designer's renovation plan is approved.* (approve)
2. Next, _____ (build)
3. Then _____ (repaint)
4. After that, _____ (install)
5. Then _____ (deliver)
6. Finally, _____ (reopen)

84 • Unit 14

15 There should be a law!

1 What should be done about each situation? Write sentences about these pictures, giving your opinion or a recommendation. Use the passive form with **should**, **shouldn't**, or **ought to**.

1. Leaving trash in the streets
2. Writing graffiti on walls
3. Playing car stereos late at night
4. Not maintaining public transportation well

1. *People shouldn't be allowed to leave trash in the streets.* OR
   People ought to be required to pick up their own trash.
2. _____
3. _____
4. _____

85

2　Give recommendations about the situations shown in these pictures. Use the passive form with have to, must, or mustn't.

1. <u>A law has to be passed to prevent people from losing their homes.</u> OR
   <u>Something must be done to repair abandoned homes.</u>
2. _____
   _____
3. _____
   _____
4. _____
   _____

3

Think of four things that you have strong opinions about. Write your opinions and explain your reasons for them. Use passive modals.

Example: *In my opinion, a four-day week should be given to everyone because people need more free time.*

1. I feel that _____

2. I think that _____

3. In my opinion, _____

4. I don't think that _____

4

Respond to these opinions by giving a different one of your own. Use expressions from the box.

> That's interesting, but I think . . .
> That's not a bad idea. On the other hand, I feel . . .
> You may have a point. However, I think . . .
> Do you? I'm not sure . . .

1. A: Mandarin Chinese is a very useful language to learn.
   B: *You may have a point. However, I think that English is more useful for traveling.*

2. A: I think having a pet makes you more relaxed.
   B: _____

3. A: Public transportation should be provided free of charge.
   B: _____

4. A: I think having a car is almost a necessity nowadays.
   B: _____

5. A: In my opinion, all plastic containers should be banned.
   B: _____

> Excuse me, could you tell us how to get to the Louvre?

There should be a law! • 87

5 Getting revenge

A Have you ever been so annoyed with a friend or neighbor that you did something to annoy him or her in return? If so, what did your friend or neighbor do? What did you do in return?

Revenge stories

1 I used to have a friend who was a lot of fun. She always loved to go out to eat together. There was just one small problem: Every time the waiter brought the check, she would say, "Uh-oh! I don't have enough money with me. Could I pay you back later?"

This was OK the first and second time it happened. But these excuses happened again and again – even for little things, like a cup of coffee or a snack after class!

So, I finally decided to get my revenge. The next time we went out for dinner, I announced that I had forgotten my wallet. She was shocked, but she paid the check. However, she has never called me to go out again. I guess she was a moocher – a person who always tries to get someone else to pay.
– Marcy, California

2 My neighbors used to keep rabbits in their yard, but they treated them very badly. Rabbit pens should be cleaned regularly, but these rabbits were very dirty, and the smell was really terrible. Worse, I noticed that the rabbits didn't have enough to eat or drink. When I complained to my neighbors, they said, "It's none of your business. They're not your rabbits, are they?"

When I called the animal protection society, they said they would investigate. I waited a week, but nothing happened. One night, I stole the rabbits and took them home. The next day I gave them to a local pet shelter.
– Jonathan, Colorado

3 I was having problems sleeping because of a dripping noise coming from my air conditioner. I thought the air conditioner needed to be repaired, so I called a technician. She couldn't find anything wrong with it, but she said the dripping was coming from the apartment above me. I asked my neighbor to have his air conditioner checked, but he said, "If you can't sleep, that's your problem!"

The following day, I climbed a ladder and attached a rubber pipe to my neighbor's air conditioner. Then I stuck the pipe through his bedroom window. The next night, my neighbor's bedroom was flooded!
– Chad, Florida

B Read the posts on an Internet site. Then complete the chart.

Problem	First attempt to solve it	Final solution
1.		
2.		
3.		

C Do you think getting revenge – doing something mean to someone in return – is a good or bad thing? Why?

88 • *Unit 15*

6 Add tag questions to these statements.

1. It isn't easy to make ends meet these days, ____is it____ ?
2. The city doesn't provide enough services for elderly people, ____does it____ ?
3. You can easily spend all your money on food and rent, _____ ?
4. Some unemployed people don't really want to work, _____ ?
5. Health care is getting more and more expensive, _____ ?
6. There are a lot of homeless people downtown, _____ ?
7. Some companies have excellent child-care services, _____ ?
8. Laws should be passed to reduce street crime, _____ ?

7 Nouns and verbs

A Complete the chart.

Noun	Verb	Noun	Verb
abolition	abolish	improvement	_____
abuse	_____	_____	insure
_____	advertise	pollution	_____
disturbance	_____	_____	provide
_____	gamble	requirement	_____

B Write eight sentences with tag questions using words from the chart. Use four of the nouns and four of the verbs.

Example: _The practice of keeping animals in cages should be abolished, shouldn't it?_

1. _____
2. _____
3. _____
4. _____
5. _____
6. _____
7. _____
8. _____

There should be a law! • 89

8 Give one reason for and one reason against these opinions.

1. Children should be made to study a foreign language in primary school.
    For: _It would help children understand other cultures._
    Against: _I don't think it would be easy to find enough teachers._

2. Literacy programs should be developed by our public schools.
    For: _____
    Against: _____

3. More tax money ought to be spent on cleaning graffiti off city walls.
    For: _____
    Against: _____

4. Stray animals should be cared for free of charge, shouldn't they?
    For: _____
    Against: _____

9 Complete the conversation. Use passive modals and tag questions.

Kate: You know, I just moved into this new apartment building, and I thought everything would be really great now.

Tony: What's the problem?

Kate: Well, yesterday, the manager gave me a copy of the house rules. I found out that I can't park my moped on the sidewalk in front of the building anymore.

Tony: But people shouldn't _____ to park their bikes or mopeds there. (permit)

Kate: Why not? There isn't any other place to park, _____ ? I guess I'll have to park on the street now.

Tony: Yes, that's too bad, but I also think people shouldn't _____ to block the sidewalk or the entrance to the building. (allow)

Kate: Well, you may have a point, but parking spaces for all types of cycles need _____ for renters here. (provide) Everyone with a car has a parking space, _____ ?

Tony: Well, yes, you're right. You should go to the next renter's meeting and discuss the issue with everyone else.

Kate: That's not a bad idea. My voice ought _____ (hear) as much as anyone else's – I think I will!

90 • Unit 15

16 Challenges and accomplishments

1 **Complete the sentences with your own ideas about the jobs in the box.**

> acting in movies   being unemployed   ✓ teaching young children
> being a student   doing volunteer work   writing for a magazine

1. One of the most rewarding aspects _of teaching young children is seeing them develop._
2. The most challenging thing _____
3. One of the rewards _____
4. One of the most difficult things _____
5. The most interesting aspect _____
6. One of the least interesting aspects _____

2 **The best and worst of it**

A Complete the chart with your own ideas.

Job	One of the best things	One of the worst things
1. social worker	_helping people_	_____
2. using a computer all day	_____	_getting eye strain_
3. running your own business	_making your own schedule_	_____
4. emergency-room nurse	_____	_working long hours_

B Write about the positive and negative aspects of the jobs in part A.

1. _One of the best things about being a social worker is helping people._
   One of the worst things is _____
2. _____
3. _____
4. _____

91

3 *Write two paragraphs about a job you find interesting. In the first paragraph, describe some positive aspects of the job. In the second paragraph, describe some of its negative aspects.*

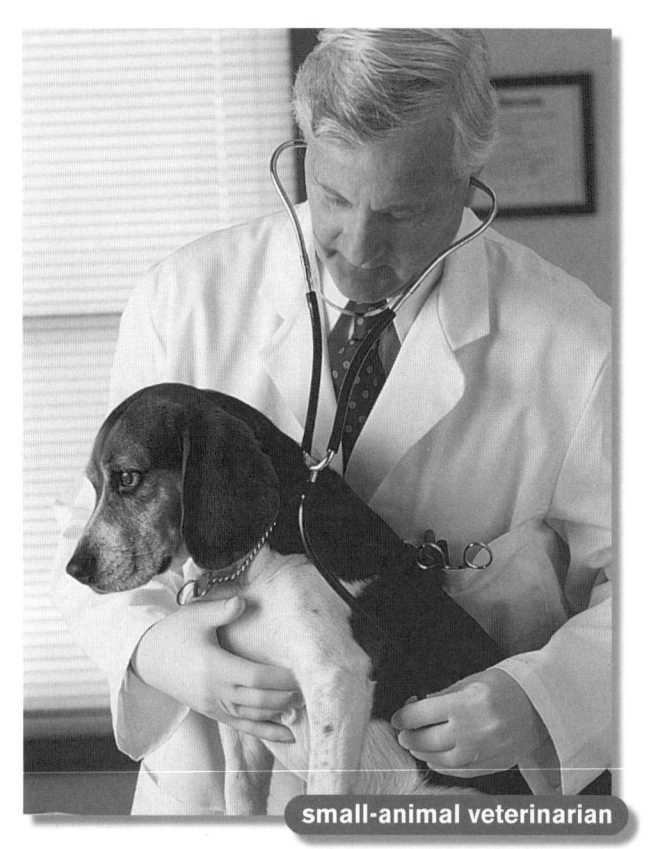

small-animal veterinarian

large-animal veterinarian

　　Being a veterinarian is both rewarding and challenging. People bring animals with different sorts of problems into the clinic every day. One of the best things about the job is treating and curing those animals that are seriously sick or injured. It's an amazing thing to be able to save an animal and bring a smile to a pet owner's face.

　　Sometimes, if an animal is very sick or badly injured, it's not possible to treat it successfully. The saddest aspect of the job is dealing with animals you cannot save. It's a terrible loss for both the vet and the pet owner.

4 Huge challenges, enormous rewards

A Have you ever done volunteer work? If so, what kind of work did you do? If not, is there any kind of volunteer work that you would like to do?

Médecins Sans Frontières

Médecins Sans Frontières (MSF), which means "Doctors Without Borders," was established in 1971. It is now the world's largest independent organization that provides emergency medical relief. Its aim is to help people who have suffered badly in wars or natural disasters, such as earthquakes or floods.

Each year, about 3,000 people are sent abroad to work in more than 70 different countries worldwide. MSF relies on volunteer professionals but also works closely with locals. In most projects, there are seven local staff members to every one foreigner. Volunteers are paid about $800 a month and receive travel expenses. They usually work for nine months to a year on a project. However, about 50 percent of volunteers go on more than one mission. One volunteer reports, "Working in politically sensitive areas with limited resources can be frustrating, but there is huge satisfaction in making even a small or temporary difference to people. What better recommendation than to say "I'm about to leave on a third mission!"

What qualities and skills do you need to become a volunteer? You have to be able to deal with stress, and you need to be able to work independently as well as in a team. You are not required to have medical qualifications. Besides medical expertise, MSF needs the skills of technical staff such as building engineers and food experts.

The reaction of volunteers returning from MSF speaks for itself. "One of my biggest challenges was organizing a team to open a new hospital in a town that had had no medical care for three years," one volunteer said. This volunteer said the project was a success because of the reduction of deaths and the fact that the local people were so thankful. Another volunteer says, "With MSF, I have had the chance to travel and test my skills to the limits both professionally and personally. The rewards can be enormous."

B Read the magazine article. What are two challenges and two rewards of volunteering?

Challenges: _____ _____

Rewards: _____ _____

C Answer the questions.

1. What is the aim of Médecins Sans Frontières?

   _____

2. How many countries receive foreign volunteers through MSF?

   _____

3. What is the average ratio of local staff members to foreign volunteers?

   _____

4. What personal qualities must volunteers have?

   _____

5. What kinds of experts does MSF require?

   _____

5 Choose the correct word.

1. If teachers are to be successful, they have to be _____ .
   (dependent / inflexible / resourceful)

2. You have to be _____ if you work as a volunteer.
   (adaptable / cynical / unimaginative)

3. If you take a job far from your family and friends, you have to be _____ .
   (compassionate / dependent / self-sufficient)

4. It's no good being _____ if you're an emergency-room nurse.
   (courageous / rigid / upbeat)

5. One of the most important things about working with children is being positive and not _____ .
   (adaptable / cynical / resourceful)

6. Being a role model for troubled youths requires someone who is strong and _____ .
   (courageous / dependent / timid)

6 Choose the correct prepositions.

☑ about ☐ by ☐ for ☐ from ☐ in ☐ of

1. One of the most exciting things _about_ working abroad is learning about another culture.

2. In the next few years, I'd like to have lived in a culture that's very different _____ my own.

3. For me, the most difficult aspect _____ working abroad is learning a foreign language.

4. Working _____ an organization like the Peace Corps is very rewarding.

5. I'd like to have gotten another degree _____ two years.

6. I hope I'll have gotten married _____ the time I'm 30.

94 • Unit 16

7 Accomplishments and goals

A Match the verbs with the nouns. Write the collocations. (More than one answer may be possible.)

Verbs	Nouns
☑ buy	☐ debts
☐ get	☑ a house
☐ learn	☐ a move
☐ make	☐ a promotion
☐ meet	☐ new skills
☐ pay off	☐ someone special

1. *buy a house*
2. _____
3. _____
4. _____
5. _____
6. _____

B Write about accomplishments and goals. Use your own information, the words in part A, and the present perfect, past simple, future perfect, or *would like to have* + past participle.

1. *My sister and her husband have managed to save enough money to buy a house. I expect to have bought a house within five years.*
2. _____
3. _____
4. _____
5. _____
6. _____

Challenges and accomplishments • 95

8 Personal portraits

A Write three sentences about the accomplishments of someone you know very well. Use the present perfect or simple past.

Example:

By carefully investing his money, my friend Paulo has been able to retire at 30. He has managed to set up an organization that helps find jobs for people who are homeless. In addition, he . . .

B Write three sentences about things the same person would like to have achieved in the next ten years. Use the future perfect or *would like to have* + past participle.

Example:

Paulo would like to have traveled a lot by the time he's 40. He hopes to have started an organization to provide scholarships for needy college students. He also hopes he'll have . . .

96 • Unit 16